LIGHT
in the Dark Belt

.

Rosa J. Young, 1949

THE STORY OF ROSA YOUNG
as told by herself

LIGHT

in the Dark Belt

·

Saint Louis, Missouri - 1950

CONCORDIA PUBLISHING HOUSE

Revised Edition

This edition published 2014 by Concordia Publishing House
3558 S. Jefferson Avenue, St. Louis, MO 63118-3968
1-800-325-3040 · www.cph.org

Text © 1950 Concordia Publishing House

Cover photo: Courtesy of Concordia Historical Institute

Manufactured in the United States of America

Route #1 Box #67,
Snow Hill, Alabama,
December 10, 1929.

Dear dear Miss Thumstedter;
Please accept my
heartfelt and sincere thanks for the invaluable package
of clothing which you sent to me for the needy people
here. They reached me safe yesterday. I dare say
that this gift of clothing will make many a
little negro kids happy. And their parents also.
The colored people, haven't much of this worlds goods
Both men, women and children are greatly in need. Please
extend to the donors of these gifts my sincere thanks,
Dear Miss Thumstedler, I am enjoying fine
fine health this fall. I am able to go out now and
work for Jesus some more. Is not that wonderful.
I love to do mission work. It is all my business
here below to tell that old old story of Jesus and
his love. Save myself and some one else, Please
write again sometime. Again I thank you.
Yours in Jesus our Savior,
Rosa I. Young

AUTHOR'S PREFACE

•

FIRST, I DEDICATE THIS BOOK TO THE YOUTH OF OUR Lutheran Church, both white and colored. The aged members of our Church are passing on. They have served their time, and, one by one, they are leaving the great commission of Jesus: "Go ye, therefore, and teach all nations, baptizing them in the name of the Father and of the Son and of the Holy Ghost" (Matt. 28:19), in the hands of the present and the future generations. It should be helpful for these young people to have a more complete knowledge of our Negro mission work in Alabama, to be informed regarding its origin, its accomplishments, and its needs.

Second, I dedicate this book to our God-given white friends in Alabama, particularly to Mr. J. Lee Bonner and Mr. J. C. Harper of Oak Hill, Mr. H. L. Bruce of Catherine, and Mr. George Cook of Rockwest; and to the memory of the late Mrs. J. Lee Bonner, Mr. J. T. Dale of Oak Hill, Mr. G. T. Wiltsie of Prairie, Mr. Dennis Forte of Buena Vista, and Ex-Governor B. M. Miller of Camden, and to their descendants.

In the early days of our mission endeavors, when help was sorely needed, these white people gave their moral and material support, which made it possible for us to organize and to extend our mission work into new places. It will be beneficial to give their descendants a clear knowledge of what the Lutheran Church, which their forefathers encouraged, has done, and is still doing, for the colored people on the plantations and in various communities. Our desire is to reach more new territories in our mission work in Alabama, and to do so we shall always need our white friends.

Last, but not least, I dedicate this book to our faithful Lutherans everywhere, who out of love for Jesus have given, and continue to give, their words of encouragement, their earnest prayers, and their money to bring the pure Gospel to the colored, many of whom are still groping in spiritual darkness. I wish it were possible for these dear Lutheran white friends to know our innermost thoughts and to understand how grateful we are for what they have done for us. We must continue to ask them to help us bring the truth of God's Word to many more of our benighted brothers and sisters in Alabama.

THE AUTHOR

CONTENTS

•

ILLUSTRATIONS

•   •

LIGHT
in the Dark Belt

.

I

LIFE IN THE BLACK BELT WHEN THE AUTHOR WAS YOUNG

•

THE AUTHOR IS WHOLLY A PRODUCT OF THE BLACK BELT OF Alabama. She was born, reared, and educated in the State, under rather adverse circumstances. She has devoted forty years of her life to serving her race as a teacher. She has served in the rural districts, on plantations, in the darkest and most dangerous nooks and corners. Her work has been among the lowly, humble people, not among those who had attended high school and college. Perhaps they had heard of "Big" Tuskegee, but not of Hampton Institute. Some of them did not even know that General Lee had surrendered *o General Grant. She lived with these people, she ate with them, drank with them, slept with them, rode and walked with them. She writes of the things which she observed and experienced among her people.

HOUSES AND HOME LIFE

Some of the houses in the Black Belt were one-room log huts with only one door and no other opening for air or light. In these huts father and mother and children lived. One room was to them bedroom, living room, storage room, bathroom, dining room, and kitchen.

There was another type of dwelling, a large one-door hut, so large that it was called the "big" house, though it could not boast of a single window. In the yard, a few feet from the "big" house, a small log hut with dirt floor was built.

This small hut was the kitchen. The "big" house was the bedroom for all, also the storage room, and the living room for the grownups. The children's living room was the yard behind the house or the kitchen if the weather was rainy or cold. The children were not allowed to go into the "big" house until night unless they were sick. If a little tot got sleepy during the day, he slept on the kitchen floor or in the yard on an old piece of quilt.

A third style of house was the log pen. A log pen consists of two rooms connected by an open hall. One room served as bedroom, living room, and storage room for the parents; the other as kitchen and children's bedroom.

The fourth type of house was more aristocratic. It consisted of one or two rooms built of planks in box fashion. They were called frame, or box, houses. If there were two rooms, they were connected by an open hall. These houses were usually whitewashed, not painted. Only people of importance in the community lived in these houses. The author, in her years of service as a teacher, was often invited to share the hospitality of these larger homes. Any of these houses, though comfortable in summer, was likely to be most uncomfortable in the winter season, because chimneys were seldom built high enough and a draft of wind would send a cloud of smoke into the room, compelling the occupants to put out the fire and shiver in the cold.

Though the houses were usually not built level with the ground, steps were almost unheard of. Once the author visited in one such home. All the members of the family were elated to see their teacher coming. The father, to show his delight, rushed to the door, with outstretched arms, to lift the teacher into the house. But she was young and able to take the step without assistance.

The furniture consisted of one or two wooden beds, scalded almost white (mute evidence of frequent battles with bedbugs), rough, homemade tables, boxes, empty nail kegs, benches, and wagon seats, to be used for chairs.

There were no mirrors. The people felt to find out whether they had their clothes on correctly, or one told another when he was dressed properly.

There were no timepieces. To tell time, most of the people watched their shadows. When the human shadow was short enough for the person's feet to touch its head, it was noon. Some listened for the big plantation bell to ring for the noon hour. Others listened for the braying of a jack, which, they believed, brayed every hour. There were others who watched the sun ascend and descend in the heavens.

There were no factory-made brooms. The women swept their floors with bunches of broom sage, a tall, bushy grass, or with the branch of a pine tree. Some used rags, especially those who lived in the one-room log huts. Those who lived in the plank, or box, house used palmetto brooms, which were made by broommakers on the plantations.

Quilts large enough to cover the bed and hang over a considerable length to make sure that all in the bed would get a share of the cover were used on the beds. There were no sheets. Some used a dirty quilt to cover the mattress, which was made of hay or pine needles. Pillows were rags or soiled clothes. There were no towels. The women wiped their hands and faces on their aprons or dress tails. The men dried their faces with their arms and wiped their hands on their trousers.

There were no cooking stoves. All cooking was done in the fireplace in iron skillets and pots. Wide pieces of tin were used for lids. Wooden trays were used for bread, gourds for dippers, pine knots for lamps. There were no washbowls or wash pans. One would pour water for another while he washed his face and hands.

The meals consisted chiefly of white bread or burned corn bread, sweet potatoes, sorghum, collard greens, bitter turnips, black-eyed peas, milk, and butter. Seldom was there a table at which the members of the family might sit down together. The food was served in tin plates, pans, buckets, or bucket lids. The members of the family sat down wherever they wished and ate with their fingers—except the few. Some said the food tasted better when eaten with the fingers.

In almost every yard a mulberry tree provided the shade. Very little cleaning was done in the house or in the yard. A sickle was seldom used on the weeds and grass. The garbage can was unknown. Peelings, seeds, corncobs, watermelon rinds, and pinder (*peanut*) hulls were all thrown into the yard. Cows, mules, goats, pigs, dogs, and chickens came and went—and snakes, too. Parts of the hall or bedroom were often used for storing piles of corn and cottonseed.

The women usually wore one-piece dresses tied around the waist with a string. They combed their hair with a table fork and tied the braids with string. Men wore their trousers rolled up halfway to the knees and held them up with one homemade suspender. All went barefoot. They did not bother to wash their feet before retiring at night, even at the end of a rainy day.

Most of the people had learned to be polite to teachers and ministers, but among themselves they were rough and uncouth. The moral status of the people was at a very low ebb. The people, ignorant of the true way of salvation, lived in spiritual darkness.

THE NEGLECT OF CHILDREN

"Suffer the little children to come unto Me, and forbid them not, for of such is the Kingdom of God. . . . And He took them up in His arms, put His hands upon them, and blessed them." (Mark 10:14-16.) The parents, instead of leading the little ones to God, their Creator, often severely neglected them both in spiritual and in temporal things.

A bath was not even a weekly experience for many colored children. Often a baby was not given a bath until after its weaning time. As the child grew older, its kinky, dirty hair became matted with cockleburs, cotton lint, and pine needles. Banks of dirt accumulated on the back of the neck, elbows, wrists, hands and feet. Fingernails were long and dirty. Yet they must eat with their fingers. As a rule the superstitious parents did not permit them to remove the fingernails, because to do so would make them roguish.

Until the girls reached the teen age, they wore only one garment. Usually there were two garments for a change, but some had only one "piece," which they wore until the mother decided it should be washed. While the washing was being done, the child went about naked. No washing was ever done in inclement weather. Some were so unfortunate as never to have a change of garment until the old one had entirely worn out. Shoes were almost an unknown luxury.

Chiefly the food consisted of a piece of corn bread, a sweet potato, and a generous helping of collard greens or peas cooked with okra with no seasoning at all. Some were less fortunate, having only cold corn bread or a roasted sweet potato, with water to drink. Sometimes, between meals, the children were given raw potatoes, parched corn, peas or rice uncooked.

Sometimes when the children were given a piece of bread for breakfast and were told they would get another piece with a glass of milk mixed with water for dinner, they would save their piece of breakfast bread until noon so that·they would have what they called a "good eat."

Mr. A. was one of the important men. He lived in a log hut with the kitchen out in the yard. Once he bought a barrel of flour and a can of lard. There was no place to put this big supply but in the big house behind the head of his bed. Mr. A. was a preacher and held family prayers each night. When the family gathered for prayers, first one and then another of the hungry children would kneel behind the bed, near the flour and lard. While the prayers were being said, it would be easy to steal a pan of flour and a cup of lard. Then the culprit would sneak out to the kitchen in the yard, and after prayers all the children would cook and eat and return to the big house to go to bed.

Some of the colored people put their little children into the field to work when they are very much too young. It seems as if the parents were charging the children for the right to live. The very small ones are given the task of picking up sticks and bringing water for the kitchen. If they fail to do their tasks, they are often whipped, and sometimes they are denied the scanty meal, while the others eat.

CHRISTMAS

Before Christmas the children were always told to clean up the house and yard if they wanted Santa Claus to come to them. Then the children would rake and sweep and carry dirt until they ached in every limb, hoping to receive something from Santa, if only a "bite." When all the cleaning was done, they went among their neighbors or kinsfolk to borrow stockings to hang up, for even the colored boys and girls must hang their stockings before the chimney. On Christmas Eve, when all were fast asleep in bed, the poor mama would put into their stockings what she had. She split an apple into halves so that each child might have a taste; the oranges were divided in like manner. To these halves she would add one or two sticks of candy and sometimes a dozen raisins. On Christmas morning the little ones would rise long before dawn to lay claim to their stockings. Oh, how happy they were! Many, many children never tasted candy, apples, or oranges except on Christmas.

RELIGIOUS TRAINING

Far below everything else was their religious training. The little colored children did not know any prayers. They did not know that God had made them. They did not know that God made the world. They did not know what was meant by a Bible verse. They did not know how to sing. They did not know what was right and what was wrong.

Only a few had ever attended church or Sunday school. They did not know what a church looked like on the inside. Their job was to stay at home and take care of the house while the grownups went to church to worship God. When a member of the family died, the children were usually left at home during the hour of the funeral. One little boy, who was taken to his little sister's burial, said, when he returned home: "I saw dem men puttin' all dot dirt on woman. Um gyin back dow da and git her up.'"

Marriages were not usually witnessed by the younger children. Mr. L. had a daughter who was about to get married. The marriage was to take place in the home. The youngsters, wondering what all this could mean, determined to see for themselves. They were put to bed long before the hour set for the wedding, but they did not go to sleep. From under

their covers they witnessed a marriage. Still they wondered
what it could mean.

They had no knowledge of the Bible. My readers can
scarcely imagine this state of affairs, for their children know
so much about Jesus; but many colored children had never
heard of Jesus. They had never heard the story of Jesus'
Passion, His innocent suffering and death, for the sins of
the world. Just think of it! They had never heard about
the scourging, the mockery, the crucifixion of Jesus. No one
had been sufficiently interested in the welfare of their souls to
tell them about the true God, that Jesus is the Son of God
and their Savior. Right here in the land of Bibles, thousands
of little black children had never seen a happy day; they
were growing up like weeds and bushes, children without
hope, without God.

SCHOOLS FOR THE COLORED CHILDREN

"Train up a child in the way he should go; and when he
is old, he will not depart from it" (Prov. 22:6).

In the light of the above Bible verse we see that the homes
had largely failed. We shall now see what the schools did for
the colored children. The school terms were short, only
three or four months during the year. Because of the short-
ness of the term the few who attended would forget most
of what they learned before time for another term to begin.

In some counties, if the colored people failed to operate a
school for one year, their share of the public school funds
would be withdrawn and distributed among the schools for
the white children.

If there was a course of study, it was not given to the
colored schools. Each teacher chose his own subjects or
permitted each child to study whatever book he might have.
The schools were not graded. Almost every child had a dif-

ferent lesson, and, as a rule, the child promoted himself. There was no schedule of time. Each teacher began and closed school according to her own convenience. Some schools were opened for the day when the majority of the children had arrived, and they were closed at the discretion of the teacher. Usually the hours in school were few.

There was little discipline. During school hours there was always some kind of disturbance, giggling, pinching, fighting; even eating and sleeping. The school could always be heard some distance away.

The Bible was never read in school, nor was a prayer offered. No Christian song was ever sung. Nor could it have been otherwise, for the teachers did not know Jesus as their Savior. They did not know the Commandments. They were not familiar with Christian hymns.

In Miss N.'s school some of the pupils' parents purchased from conjurers small articles which the conjurers claimed would help the children to master their lessons and prevent the teacher from punishing them. A child possessing one of these articles, called a "hand," would not dare to enter the schoolroom without it. If he had, by chance, forgotten the "hand," he would walk home to get it, even though he might be tardy. This was more important than the Lord's Prayer or a Bible verse. Such things should be left to the Church, according to the opinion of parents and school officials. Therefore much of the learning that was secured was worse than no learning.

TEACHERS

Most of the public school teachers in those days were inefficient, incapable, not knowing much more than those whom they were trying to teach. Many secured their positions by bribery; some, through friendship with officials;

others occupied the teacher's chair solely because of the negligence of the school authorities. Usually the pupils and teacher had to study together. The pupils consulted the speller to see whether they had spelled the words correctly; so did the teacher. The pupils had to look up the capitals of the different States; the teacher had to do the same. The pupils did not know the simplest rules of grammar; neither did the teacher. The pupils had to read their multiplication tables from the arithmetic; so did the teacher. As a result of this kind of teaching, thousands of children were growing up without learning to read and write and spell.

The teachers of that day accepted meager salaries. They were paid from $12.50 to $18.75 a month. Teacher N. taught a school in Escambia County for $4.50 a month. But most of the teachers were trying, though in a most pitiable way, to help their race.

School Buildings and Equipment

There were no school buildings. Schools were conducted in the local churches. There were no stoves. During the cold weather, fires were kindled in the churchyard. Then the teacher not only had to try to teach, but to watch the fire and the little raggedy pupils.

For school desks the long benches in the church were used. The child kept his books beside him on the seat. He used his lap for a writing desk. Blackboards were made of rough planks dyed with ink. When no plank could be found, the teacher measured off a space on the church wall and colored it with ink. All pupils were required to bring a penny or one egg to pay for the crayon.

The same kind of broom that was used in the home was used for the school.

Water was carried in a wooden pail from a near-by spring. The children drank from their hands or from their lunch-bucket lid.

HYGIENE

Children came to school wearing the same clothes they wore at home, dirty, greasy, stiff with sorghum, full of holes, buttons off, trouser legs ripped to the knee, hems out of the girls' dresses. Faces and hands were dirty; hair was uncombed. Ventilation was a necessity alone from this angle.

RECREATION ON THE PLANTATION IN THE DARK BELT

"The people sat down to eat and to drink and rose up to play" (Ex. 32:6).

Recreation is good for all; yet if it is not conducted in a decent manner, it is harmful to all. The following chapter brings you a description of the amusement and merrymaking of the colored folk in the Dark Belt.

On Saturday nights the people held wild, sinful frolics and lewd dances, which claimed the souls of thousands. Many, many poor souls were madly, blindly reaching out after the fleeting joys and pleasures of this transient world, not knowing the one thing needful, Jesus' Word.

Before the merrymaking, or frolic, took place, all the beds, and whatever else there might have been in the room, were taken down and set outside. A bright fire was kindled on the hearth. Then a musician would come forward with his banjo, harp, fiddle, or guitar and take his seat on a chair or bench. At the first sound of the instrument the people were on their feet ready for the dance. Such dancing! Old men, old women, young men and women, boys and girls—trembling, bowing, bending, stamping, laughing, and yelling. This frenzied dance would usually last until the dawn of

Sunday morning, unless some base, ill-bred fellow started shooting and cursing. This excitement would scatter the crowd. Having accomplished their purpose, these ill-bred fellows would put out the pine-knot light on the hearth, rob the refreshment table of the food, escape into the near-by woods, and devour the food. The frolic for that night was over.

When no music could be provided, the guests would range themselves in a circle around the bare room; then all would start stamping one foot on the floor, clapping their hands together and then on their hips, snapping their fingers, all going through the same motions simultaneously.

Sometimes frolics were conducted on Saturday afternoon and all night. Someone would go to a near-by town, rent a pair of drums, and return to drum up all the people in the community. Men, women, and ragged children would assemble. For several hours they would march along the roadside, whooping and yelling until their bodies were wet with perspiration. Then they would march to someone's house for a nightlong "jamboree."

Christmas was a time for merrymaking, cooking, eating, dancing, drinking, and even fighting. A hog was always killed for Christmas if it could be afforded. All must have fresh meat. That seemed to be a necessary part of the Christmas celebration. All who could would buy jugs of beer and whisky. Even the children were given a drink. The elders claimed that the blood had to be "heated up" before they could enjoy Christmas. Frequently this Christmas reveling went on for a week, both day and night. There was horse racing, mule racing, ox racing, foot racing, wrestling, back stepping, ditch jumping, rope jumping, dog fighting, rooster fighting, and what not. "It is Christmas," the reveler would say. "Christmas don't come but once a year. If I get drunk, don't nobody care."

Christmas time was a dangerous time. Quiet, self-respecting people remained indoors for fear of being shot down by a drunken passer-by. Many lost limbs and some their lives. Many, too, lost all their money through gambling and drinking.

The Fourth of July was also a great day of rejoicing. Most of the land masters would kill a beef and divide it with the people gratis. Some of the landowners prepared meals and fed their colored folk in their back yard. When the cow was eaten up at the end of this great day, the people went back to the fields.

Both sinners and the professed Christians participated in these frolics. All joined together in the sins of cursing, stealing, envy, hatred, drunkenness, lying, and adultery. Sin ruled in the hearts of these people.

2

CHURCHES AND THEIR MODE
OF WORSHIP

*

*"For, behold, the darkness shall cover the earth
and gross darkness the people."*
Is. 60:2

*

Scattered throughout the Black Belt are many churches. Even in the days when most of the events told in this volume transpired, nearly every community had a church—a Methodist or a Baptist church or, in many sections, both. These churches did not offer the people the pure Gospel. Their form of religion was not taken from the Scriptures, but was obtained from the mourner's bench, the cemetery, the forest, the fields, the byroads, and from dreams, visions, and voices.

The mourner's bench was then, and still is, considered by many to be an essential factor in regeneration. Therefore several benches are always left vacant for mourners.

Mourners are those who are seeking religion, and during the period of seeking they are instructed to refrain from taking food and drink, combing their hair, bathing, changing their clothes, or greeting their friends; instead, they must bear a sad countenance and remain alone. Sometimes a person occupying a seat on the mourner's bench would prostrate himself on the floor. Such a person was said to have fallen under conviction. In such case the service would continue through the night if necessary, and all who could

14

remain were asked to do so in order to assist the mourner in attaining his goal, "to get religion."

Sometimes the prostrated person, as if to relieve himself from his uncomfortable position, would suddenly spring to his feet and cry out: "I got it, I got it. Thank God, I got it!" Then all the people would yell together: "Tell it, tell it. God-tol-mity, tell it." Upon this testimony the candidate was baptized and received into the church.

Suddenly one might come from the cemetery, screaming: "I found Jesus. I found Jesus, I stayed all night in the graveyard, and I wuz scared." This testimony, too, makes the candidate eligible for Baptism and for church fellowship.

Another awakes from sleep and reports that he saw a white man writing with a gold pencil; this white man wrote his name and told him to "go in peace and sin no more." Since his name had been recorded by a white man, this man would be baptized and received into the church.

The forest seeker should not be overlooked. Therefore let us hear his experience: "I seen a bird come flying by me, and I said: 'Lord, if I got de religion, let dat bird stop in dat tree.' De bird flew right up to de tree and lighted." How dare such an experience be denied—stopping a bird! He, too, would be admitted into the church.

Another experience from one walking along the road: From behind he heard a noise. Turning about to look and to listen, the candidate reports that he saw Death fast approaching on a pale horse. He ran and hid himself among the tall bushes. Death saw him, but continued on his journey down the road. This, too, was sufficient for church fellowship.

One man came from the forest and reported that, bowed in prayer, he was begging God to take his life and send him to hell. He testified: "God killed me dead and sent me to hell, but a voice called from the treetops: 'Your sins are forgiven, your soul set free. Go and tell the world what a dear Savior you have found.'" This man was licensed to preach.

Another preacher testified that a great dinner was being served. Many guests were at the table. He was sitting at the head. Suddenly a white man approached the table and placed both hands on his head and announced to all the guests: "This is the preacher." All the church members agreed that the man was thus called to preach. Forthwith he was licensed and ordained to be a preacher. They believe a man must have a similar experience before he can become a preacher.

In a church service in one of these churches only the preacher possessed a hymnbook. He would rise and with a loud voice line out a hymn, such as the one that follows:

> Father, I stretch my hand to Thee,
> No other help I know.

The people would start singing:

> Dey, hey, ley, mey, sey, fey, dey, hey
> Hey, rey, sey, fey, ey, dey.

The preacher would line out the next two verses:

> If Thou withdraw Thyself from me,
> Oh, whither shall I go?

And again they all sang as they sang the first two lines, and so on, until the hymn was ended. Then came the sermon, as they called it. Words can scarcely picture that part of the service. A collection always followed. Then the people joined hands and began shouting and going round

and round until the dust and odor of perspiration compelled them to stop.

The people were blind. They did not know what was
right and what was wrong. Darkness had covered the earth
and gross darkness the people.

3

MY EARLY LIFE

•

*And it shall come to pass, that before they call, I will answer; and
while they are yet speaking, I will hear.*

Is. 65:24

•

THE STORY OF MY LIFE MUST BE READ AND UNDERSTOOD IN
the light of the background which I have described in Chapter 1. Life in the Dark Belt was my life until God called me
to the special service in His kingdom which I have been
privileged to perform these many years.

I was born at Rosebud, in Wilcox County, Ala., May 14,
1890, in a church that stood on a plot of land about one
mile from the present site of our oldest Lutheran mission
in Alabama. My parents were Grant and Nancy Young,
devout Christians and very dutiful in church attendance.
My father was an African Methodist pastor for about twenty
years, my mother a woman of high morals. Much credit is
given to her by all who know her for the manner in which
she reared her family of ten children. We can never forget
her teachings. My deceased sister thanked mama on her
deathbed for the way she had reared us.

I am the fourth of the ten children. I dare say it will
sound strange to you to learn that I was born in a church.
I shall explain.

They tell me that on the plot of land where I was born
there was once located an African Methodist church, near
the residence of Mr. J. Lee Bonner's father. The Bonner

family could not rest during the services held in this church
on Sunday nights. The members of the church made too
much noise, shouting, hallooing, clapping their hands, and
stamping their feet. Thereupon Mr. Bonner worked out a
plan to rid himself and his family of this church. He sold
the plot of land on which it stood to one of his friends.
This friend persuaded my grandfather to buy the land, and
thus the church and the land became grandfather's.

Just about this time my father and mother were looking
for a house, and grandpa permitted them to move into the
church and make their home there. How long they lived
there I do not know, but my parents told me that I was
born in that church.

I am unable to tell much about my early youth. As long
as I can remember, I would tell all who asked me that I
was going to be a teacher. One of the first things I can remember is that we lived in a log hut and that I had a blue-
backed speller. I do not know whether I was taught or
whether I learned anything in my speller, but I clearly remember that I lost my book and grieved over this a long
time. Afterwards I found the lost book in a deep crack of
the wall of the log house and rejoiced over it.

In due time I was sent to school, and I completed the
alphabet class the first day I went to school. The name of
the teacher was Brice Hines. He placed me in the alphabet
class and took me out the same day. That did not take place
very often, for it generally took the average pupil two years
to learn the alphabet in those days, so I am told. After that
day in Brice Hines's school I do not remember whether I
continued in school or not; but the next thing I remember
is that I had another spelling book, *Patterson's Speller,* and
that I attended night school with the older children. We went

to my grandfather's house, where Mitchell Young, my father's brother, a student of Tuskegee Institute, instructed us.

I do not know how long I studied with Mitchell Young or what became of him. The next account that I can give of myself after having lost sight of Mitchell Young was that I had no teacher. I had only one book, and that was the Bible. I remember well that I would sit for hours all by myself and read the Bible. Besides reading the Bible, I would pray often. Mother taught me the Lord's Prayer with a switch. She also taught me my first recitation. The following is part of it, all that I can remember:

> 1. A little child who loves to pray
>   And read the Bible, too,
> Shall rise above the skies one day
>   And sing an angel adieu.
>
> 2. Shall live in heaven, that world above . . .

This poem had a great deal to do with my reading of the Bible and praying so often, for I wished to be one of those little children who would someday rise above the sky and sing an angel's farewell and live in heaven, that world above. Those last lines lingered in my little heart; but I had set out in the wrong way to win what I longed for by just reading the Bible and praying. I did not know that I could not read the Bible and pray enough to win heaven. My poor soul was started on the wrong road to heaven in its very childhood.

The first hymn that I could sing I learned from my two older sisters, Flora and Ida. They had learned it in Sunday school. I remember the first verse was as follows:

> Can it be right for me to go
>   On in this dark, uncertain way?
> Yet I believe and do not know
>   Whether my sins are washed away.

That hymn was misleading. The poet says he believes, and still he says that he does not know that his sins are washed away. He should have known that, for the Bible tells us that all our sins are washed away by the blood of Jesus Christ, the Son of God. So you can see that my poor soul was in darkness, groping blindly for salvation.

I do not know how long I was at home studying the Bible, and that without a teacher. My next recollection is that I was sent back to school and made the fifth grade the first day I entered this school. The teacher was a certain Prof. D. L. House, a graduate of Hampton Institute, Hampton, Va. He was my teacher often from then on until I entered the college at Selma. I never studied the first, second, or fourth-grade books. I studied the Webster blue-backed and Patterson spellers and the Bible and then entered the fifth grade. From that time on I was in regular attendance at the public schools. I loved to go to school and hardly missed a day. No matter how cold, hot, or wet it was, I went to school unless sickness prevented me from going. Even during the seasons when we had to work on the farm, I scarcely missed a day. I would rise early in the morning, go to the field, work until the first bell rang, hastily change to school-clothes, and arrive at school in time. After school I would change my clothes again and return to the field to work until nightfall. I really enjoyed the farm work and always tried to outdo my brothers in whatever work we undertook.

I soon became the family teacher, teaching all the younger children at home every night. They did not attend school. I think my teaching must not have been too bad, as my brother Sheffield Lorenz, who never attended public school, but whom I taught from the time he became of school age, made the seventh grade when he entered Snow Hill Institute, Ala.

During this period of my life I was sickly, suffering with rheumatism. At one time I was helpless for eight weeks, and after that I had to walk with a crutch for over a year. All the neighbors said I would hardly be able to walk again; but the Lord restored me to my former health. After that the neighbors, both white and colored, advised my parents to continue sending me to school and to give me an education, saying I was industrious and apt as a scholar, but not strong physically. All these sayings helped to encourage my parents to send me to high school.

I was baptized and received into the African Methodist Church in 1900, at the age of ten years. The first Sunday that I remember ever going to church, I was "converted." Prior to this time I had always been obliged to stay at home on Sundays with the smaller children and to take care of them. Papa was always busy attending to his church work, while mama and the three older children attended Sunday school and church every Sunday. The morning of that Sunday on which I attended church for the first time, I was playing out in the yard with the other children. My mother called me and asked me whether I wanted to go to church. I said I did. So I went into the house and was dressed for church. I listened very attentively to the preacher, a Rev. S. P. Inge. He had been conducting revival meetings, and this was the closing Sunday. His text was part of the seventeenth verse of the twenty-first chapter of Genesis: "What aileth thee, Hagar?" The emotional old preacher worked upon the emotions of the people as he pleaded the cause of Christ, and every time he would come down, he exclaimed, "O Hagar, what aileth thee?" The words of that passage of Holy Scripture lodged in my heart that day. It seemed as if the old preacher were talking directly to me, and to me only. He made me feel as if everyone else were doing exactly what God willed them to do except me and that he was pleading with me to do God's will. I well remember how those words rang in my heart.

After he had finished preaching, he sang two hymns. The first one was as follows:

> 1. Come, ye that love the Lord,
>   And let your joys be known,
> Join in a song with sweet accord.
> Join in a song with sweet accord.
>   And thus surround the throne,
>   And thus surround the throne.

> 2. Let those refuse to sing
>   Who never knew our God;
> But children of the heav'nly King,
> But children of the heav'nly King,
>   May speak their joys abroad,
>   May speak their joys abroad.

The first two lines of the second stanza struck me: "Let those refuse to sing who never knew our God." I saw right there that I could not sing them; so I was still.

The next hymn he sang was the following:

> I am bound for the Promised Land,
>   Who will come and go with me?
> I am bound for the Promised Land,
>   Who will come and go with me?

I remember well how all the way home, as I walked along behind my mother and sisters, the words of the text rang in my heart: "Hagar, what aileth thee? O Hagar, what aileth thee?" In the dead hours of that night I lay in my bed, weeping until my pillow was wet, praying the Lord's Prayer—all that I knew. I felt that I was treating God worse than all the other people. It seemed as though my heart would burst for sorrow because I had not done right. Every time I awoke during the night, I wept and prayed myself to sleep again, and I always heard the words of that text ringing in my heart: "Hagar, what aileth thee?"

The next morning—at least it was one Monday morning of the year 1900—I had an experience that was similar to that of other African Methodists who had been "converted." The Holy Ghost came upon me, and I was filled with the Spirit. I broke and ran into the room to prevent any of the family from hearing or seeing me cry. I said, "I have got religion, but I am not going to tell anybody." The devil shot his arrows into my heart, saying, "Don't you tell it; they will laugh at you. They will not believe you. You will have to give up all the games you have been playing." I decided not to tell. I sneaked off to the field. While at work, the Holy Ghost moved in my heart. Again I heard the words of the text: "Hagar, what aileth thee?" I burst into tears and cried out, "I have got religion. My sins are forgiven." The children screamed with laughter. I rushed home to my mother, the children following behind me and laughing. I told mama that I had religion. She made the children stop laughing. Then I went to grandmother, and when I told her, she cried. I told my sisters. They mocked, "Rosa got religion the first time she went to church!"

The preacher had closed his revival meetings that Sunday. All the new members gained through his revival had been taken into the church. I desired to go to church again and be baptized, and fellowshiped, but mother never said a word about my going to church again, and I was afraid to ask her. I did not know what to do. I waited and waited. Each Sunday I lingered, listening for some one to say something about going to church. At last I began to pray, asking the Lord to help me to get to church, so that I could be baptized. I remember well how I prayed and kept on praying, until one morning I heard my mother tell sister Flora to go to the store and get two dress patterns, as she wished to make Viola and Rosa some dresses, so that they could go to church. Oh, my heart jumped for joy, and I said, "The Lord has answered my prayer!"

Shortly after this I was taken to church one Sunday morning, and the pastor baptized me. He announced that he would have me fellowshiped into the church that night; but I was never fellowshiped into the Methodist Church because my mother did not tell me to return to church in the evening.

I had a second experience. I wished to see many strange things and hear voices, as I had heard other people say they had seen and heard when they were "converted." I began to doubt that I had got religion and started to pray again, asking the Lord to show me plainly whether I was converted. I continued to pray and pray, listening for strange voices or waiting to see strange sights.

One day I went to my grandmother's house. She told me to come to her and asked me where that religion was that I told her I had got some time ago. I began to tremble with fear, for I did not know what she would say. At last I replied in a low tone of voice, "I have it." When I looked at her, she was crying, and through her tears she said, "Something continues to reason in my heart, saying, 'Talk to that child, talk to that child.' " So she left her work and had a long religious talk with me. I left her home rejoicing.

From that time on I attended Sunday school and church
regularly. I now began to use prayer in everything I undertook. Prayer was, or seemed to have become, a part of my
life.

4

MORE SCHOOLING

●

O Thou that hearest prayer, unto Thee shall all flesh come.
Ps. 65:2

●

WHEN I COMPLETED MY ELEMENTARY EDUCATION IN THE
public schools, the Lord gave me a strong desire for a higher
education. There is no good thing within us; all good things
without and within us come from God. The words of the
Bible verse: "If ye shall ask anything in My name, I will do
it" (John 14:14), seemed to have been written in large
print upon my heart; for whenever I wanted anything or
undertook anything, I prayed to God for it. When matters
went wrong in the home with me or any other member of
the family, I would steal away and talk to Jesus about it.
I believed in prayer, prayer, prayer. Prayer will bring you
things which nothing else will or can give you. Being a
great believer in prayer, I went to the Lord and asked Him
to give me a higher education. I even vowed to the Lord
that if He would give me a higher education, I would serve
Him with it. This I prayed almost incessantly.

The Lord did hear and answer my prayer when His
time came. "Mine hour is not yet come," the Savior, on one
occasion, said to Mary (John 2:4). These words are meant
for all believers. The Savior wants to teach us that He will
help us when His time comes, no sooner, no later; but He will
give us what we ask of Him in plenty of time for us to use it
to best advantage. Never can a Christian say of Jesus that
He sent him help, but that it was too late.

27

As I said before, the Lord did answer my prayer, and this is how. There lived near our old home at Rosebud a very fine white family, Mr. J. C. Harper, his mother, sister, and brother. When we were young children, living in the country, our parents would often allow us together with the other colored people of the community, to help Mr. Harper, and he would always pay us well for our work.

One day while I was picking cotton in one of Mr. Harper's cotton patches, a little ahead of the other pickers, singing to myself the following little plantation song: "Give me Jesus, give me Jesus; you may have all this world, give me Jesus," Mr. Harper came riding along on a big red saddle horse. Looking down upon me, he said: "Rosa, your people ought to educate you; they sure ought to give you an education. You are teaching these other children how to work. You teach them in their books at night, too, don't you?" I answered, "Yes, sir." Then he rode away, saying something to himself which I did not understand. When evening came, I went home and told my parents what Mr. Harper had said. Soon after this it became the common talk among the various relatives that I should be sent to high school.

I was highly pleased with this and felt greatly uplifted in spirit. I gained fresh courage to pray for a higher education. The Lord moved the hearts of my parents, and they fully decided to send me to high school. I was a happy, happy soul. The question then arose which school I was to attend, the Snow Hill Normal and Industrial Institute at Snow Hill or Payne University at Selma. As Payne University was our church school at that time, it was soon decided to send me to Payne.

It may be interesting to know that Payne University was founded by Bishop D. A. Payne and that he was once a Lutheran. One day, in a conversation with the late Rev. Nils J. Bakke, shortly after he had begun his mission-work in Alabama, he asked me where I had been educated. I told him at Payne University. He said: "I wonder whether that school is named for Daniel." "I do not know, sir," I replied. "They called him Bishop D. A. Payne." Rev. Bakke started in surprise as if he would spring from his chair, while his face flushed and glowed like a live coal.

"That is Daniel! That is Daniel!—D. A. Payne. He was a Lutheran. Daniel was reared in the Lutheran Chruch and educated at Gettysburg Seminary, Gettysburg, Pa. (General Synod.) When he graduated in 1823, they did not have any work for him to do among the colored people. He went about preaching on the streets, and finally they lost sight of him; he drifted away."

According to the history of the African Methodist Church, Bishop Payne drifted into this church shortly after Richard Allen, its founder, severed his relations with the white Methodist Episcopal Church. Bishop Payne was a great man in the African Methodist Church. He was considered the most devout bishop in the Church and was called the Apostle of Education. He founded twenty-six schools for that Church.

Payne University, which offers a high school course, is located in the city of Selma, not many blocks from our present Alabama Lutheran Academy. In those days, in this section of the country, the majority of the people who lived in the country never visited the city, and the city people seldom came to the country; so there was practically no communication between the country folks and the city people.

However, as the Lord was pleased to have it, there was a certain Mrs. Ellen Hunt, an old friend and playmate of my father's, who, some years previous, had moved from the vicinity of our old home to West Selma. My father told me to write Mrs. Hunt and ask her whether I could board with her; for at that time there were no dormitories at Payne University. With a happy heart I soon had my letter written, and it was sent to the post office.

What was to be done next? I did not see anything for me to do but pray. I earnestly besought the Lord to make Mrs. Hunt willing to give me shelter in her home. Several weeks passed, and we heard nothing. When the Lord's time came, Mrs. Hunt answered my letter. She said she could not take me, but she had secured a nice boarding place for me with her dear old friends Nathan and Fanny Pullum.

My heart leaped for joy when I read that. Mrs. Pullum urged my father to bring me at once, as the school had already opened.

When the time came for us to leave, father did not have to buy very much for me. Through the help of the Lord I had picked cotton and made money enough to buy all my books, pay my fare to Selma, and buy all my clothes. Please remember that in those days school children did not have as many clothes as the school children do these days, nor were the clothes so expensive.

One night in the fall of 1903—I do not remember the month—papa and I boarded the train at the Allenton station en route for Payne University. After a ride of a few hours we arrived in Selma. Mrs. Hunt met us at the station. She greeted us kindly as we alighted from the coach of the train. Father introduced me to her, and soon bidding us good night, he went to the meeting place of his conference, which was in session at that time. The old city was lighted up, and my childish eyes gazed with great amazement at the bright scene as we walked along Broad Street as far as the city clock, where we turned down Dallas Street for West Selma. Everything was strange to me. It seemed as if I had been caught up in the air and placed down again in an altogether different world. Mrs. Hunt took me to her home, where I was to spend my first night in Selma.

When I awoke the next morning, there stretched before my eyes another amazing scene: fine houses of different colors, paved sidewalks, beautiful trees, grass, and flowers. It was quite different from the log huts, cabins, cottages, fields, and woods I was accustomed to see at my home in the country. After breakfast, Mrs. Hunt accompanied me to Mrs. Fanny Pullum's home. Then she took me to one Mr. John Henry Williams, who lived on Dallas Street. Here I was to join the Williams children and go to school with them every morning, as I did not know the way from West Selma to Payne University at that time. The Williams family received me kindly, and shortly we were off to school, hurrying merrily along the streets. Soon we arrived at the campus of Payne University, the place where I had longed to go and where I had so fervently and earnestly prayed the Lord to let me study.

Jesus had watched over me from infancy, had brought me to this stage in my life, and enabled me to stand upon the campus of this high school. I feel heartily sorry that because of the gross darkness in my soul and my ignorance of God's holy Word at that time I was unable to recognize the almighty hand of God and to receive my daily bread with thanksgiving, as I should have done. It was God who was doing all this for me out of pure fatherly, divine goodness and mercy, without any merit or worthiness in me. Sad to say, I was in the dark and could not see it as I do now. It was not until I was instructed in "Luther's doctrine pure" that I could really see God in everything, that I could see God in the wonderful miracles which He does for His Church, His elect.

It is a great thing to be a Christian, and this, too, I have learned since I became a Lutheran. "I will instruct thee and teach thee in the way which thou shalt go; I will guide thee with Mine eye" (Ps. 32:8).

God Will Take Care of You

Be not dismayed, whate'er betide,
   God will take care of you;
Beneath His wings of love abide—
   God will take care of you.

God will take care of you,
   Through every day o'er all the way;
He will take care of you;
   God will take care of you.

All that you need He will provide,
   God will take care of you;
Nothing you ask will be denied—
   God will take care of you!

No matter what may be the test,
   God will take care of you;
Lean, weary one, upon His breast—
   God will take care of you!

ſ

MY LIFE AT PAYNE UNIVERSITY

•

Ask, and it shall be given you; seek, and ye shall find; knock,
and it shall be opened unto you.
MATT. 7:7

•

To EXPERIENCE CRUEL, HARSH, AND UNKIND TREATMENT
amid immense obstacles has been no strange ·thing to me since
I started on life's rough sea. The first day I attended Payne
University I met with a host of discouragements. There were
assembled about two hundred students. They laughed and
mocked me because I came from the country. There were no
other children from the country attending the institution at
that time. The whole body of city children ridiculed me until
the Williams children, who had accompanied me, became
ashamed of me, with the exception of one of the girls,
Gracie. She remained a friend to me from that time on until
her death.

After much embarrassment, Gracie and I went to the
office of the president, who was Professor C. H. Henderson
of Wilberforce University, Wilberforce, Ohio. Upon first
sight he made the impression of being a good man. Mrs.
A. Wells Henderson, his wife, was an able woman; there was
no question about her scholarship; she was versed in science
and in languages. There were also four young ladies in the
faculty.

After registration I took the examination for the seventh
grade and passed it. The high grade I obtained made no
impression on the city children; instead, it seemed to arouse

33

enmity. For a whole month the entire body of students made it very unpleasant for me. I cried every day. I felt like a stranger in a distant land, without a home, friends, or money. I longed for my old country school and would have attempted to run away if I had had the money; but after buying my books I had only one dollar left.

Now, what was I to do but pray? I remembered how I had prayed to get there and how the Lord had answered my prayers. So I resorted to the same tried means that had brought me success before. There were three things I did almost incessantly: I studied, I cried, and I prayed. In the course of time I made friends with other students.

Owing to conditions at home, I was obliged to leave school that year two months before it closed. All regretted to see me leave. Some of those same children who had mocked me when I entered, wept when I left.

When I arrived home, I was greeted by all my old friends, both white and colored. During my vacation I attended Sunday school and church at the Rosebud Methodist Church and helped my parents on the farm. Our farm was three or four miles from our home. We had to leave early in the morning and did not return until night. At noon we sat down to lunch beneath a large elm tree on the bank of Pursley Creek. I carried my books along with me in a sack each day as if I were going to school. After lunch I would steal away a short distance down stream from the crowd, where I would lie down on the bank of the creek and study and pray for the remainder of the noon hour.

That fall I picked cotton for Mr. Harper again in order to help get my things for school: clothes, shoes, money for books, and the railroad fare to Selma. The Lord blessed my efforts. God, out of pure fatherly, divine goodness, enabled me to re-enter Payne. I was welcomed by all—schoolmates, classmates, teachers, and friends. I was one month behind the class; however, I mastered the situation very well because I had studied all those lessons down on the banks of the Pursley Creek during the summer.

By the help of the Lord everything went well with me that term. My work in the classroom was satisfactory. We organized the following societies, of which I was elected president and re-elected four consecutive years: the Allen League, the Loyal Temperance League, and the Payne Literary Society. There was one discouragement which I had to face that year. My parents shipped my eatables, such as they raised on the farm, to me monthly. I had to go to the freight house and be identified to get them. It was indeed embarrassing for me to go there among those rough-looking men, with so many horses and wagons around. I really dreaded the days when I had to go there.

One day, as I was coming out of the freight house, I met a drayman, Mr. Robert Boyd. He asked me what my name was. I told him it was Rosa Young. He then asked me why I came there every month. I explained the situation to him, telling him that I was a student in the school, and as my parents had no money to purchase my food at my boarding place, they sent me every month such supplies as they raised on the farm. He did not say any more, but from that time, whenever he saw a box or sack marked Rosa Young, he would pay the freight and bring it out to me. This same Mr. Robert Boyd who hauled my freight when I was a girl later hauled freight for our Lutheran mission in Selma.

That year I again had to leave school before it closed. When I arrived home, I was welcomed by all my old friends as before. That vacation was spent practically the same way as the one of the previous year.

The third year at Payne (1905-06) was a difficult year. I call it the year of hardships. In the first place, there was a new corps of teachers, and they took nothing for granted; a student had to pass or repeat the work. That year we had a new president, Professor J. M. Henderson of Detroit, Michigan. It was said of him that he had gone to school twenty-five years and that he had five different diplomas.

When I first saw President Henderson, I thought he was the finest specimen of a man, physically, mentally, and spiritually, that I had ever seen. The other teachers for the Normal Department were Prof. J. L. Henderson of Morris Brown College, Atlanta, Ga.; his son, Prof. W. H. Bowen of Canada; and Mrs. A. Wells Henderson, the wife of our ex-president C. H. Henderson.

Secondly, I was a month behind in my work, as they had already taken up those high branches of science that are taught in the Normal Department. Mrs. A. Wells Henderson was kind enough to help me with my back work at night. I would walk across the town every evening to the place where Mrs. Henderson was boarding, recite my back lessons, then return to my room and prepare my lessons for the next day. In addition to that, I had to study the lessons in advance in order to be able to make my class before school closed, because I was obliged to leave school every year before it closed. Therefore I studied till twelve and one o'clock every night.

Thirdly, owing to illness in the Pullum family, I had to find a new home. I went to Mrs. N. N. She was the meanest woman I have ever seen. I had to get up before daylight, strip the beds, hang out the bedding, scrub the floor, take in the bedding, cook breakfast, and wash before school every morning. Once I became sick there for a few days. I could not lie in bed during the day. I had to lie on a chair and across my trunk. "Aunt" N. N. stole my groceries, and I would partly have to starve the remainder of the month. She would steal my kerosene, and I would have to lie prostrate before the fireplace and study my lessons by the light of the coals in the grates. I prayed almost incessantly to the Lord to grant me strength to hold on. The Lord did help me, but, as usual, I had to leave for home before the school closed.

That summer I worked but three months on the farm. I taught a private school in the Rosebud Methodist church and was enabled to buy all the things necessary for school and my railroad fare to Selma and had enough money to pay my first month's board.

At the beginning of my fourth year at Payne (1906 to 1907) I found a boarding place with Mrs. Maggie Austin. There conditions were more pleasant for me. During that term we published a monthly paper, the *Payne Sentinel,* of which I was chosen editor. The president also appointed me subteacher for the university. Meanwhile I was reviewing for the State examination. The above-mentioned duties required much of my time, and besides I had to prepare my daily classwork. All this mental work was very taxing. That December I passed my first State examination, and during the summer I taught my first public school at Oleo, Ala., near our present-day mission at Vredenburgh.

At the beginning of my fifth year at Payne (1907 to 1908) I moved to the home of Mrs. Lara Gracie, a widow. She was a kind old "mammy"; I called her "Mama" Grace and continued to board with her every year until I finished school.

That term I won two prizes, a gold medal in an oratorical contest and the five-dollar prize in the mathematical contest. That year saw my first commencement exercises at Payne. During my vacation that summer I went to Mulberry, Ala., where I taught my second public school.

The sixth year at Payne (1908-09) was my senior year. This was indeed a year of hard mental work. I was a Sunday school teacher at Brown's Chapel, A. M. E. Church, subteacher at the school, president of the societies of our school, editor of the *Payne Sentinel,* and president of the senior class. The class asked me to select for them the class color, flower, and motto and to compose the class song. After praying over the matter, I made the following selection: —

> Class color: Steel gray
> Class flower: Carnation.
> Class motto: "Serve as You Go."
> Class song: "We have started today on life's journey,
>   Alone on the highway of life, etc."

I presented these to the class. They were well received and accepted.

On Easter Sunday I was on the program to read an essay, the subject of which was "The Value of the Bible." The reading of this essay made a good impression, and the audience requested that it be published. I had the essay printed in pamphlet form, and it sold rapidly around Selma. I gave the proceeds to the school.

My work was so strenuous that year that I had a nervous breakdown just a few weeks before commencement. I had to deliver my graduation oration while seated.

June 1, 1909, is a day I shall never forget. It was the day of my graduation. Long before ten o'clock in the morning the eager audience had filled the chapel. There were five in my class, and we all spoke. The names of the graduates, together with the titles of their essays, were as follows:

 Mr. E. L. Henderson, "The Ideal Man."—Salutatorian.
 Miss Martha O. Brown, "The Battle of Life."
 Miss Viola Mae Young (my sister), "Labor Conquers."
 Mr. Chas. Hooks, "The Young Afro-American."

I was the last one to speak, being the valedictorian. My subject was "Serve the People." This was my address:

SERVE THE PEOPLE

There rests upon mankind a moral obligation, the highest law, by which they are mutually bound to aid each other. This is the highest conception of duty both to God and man.

The demand of the civilized world has ever been for efficient service, and the man who has learned the art of serving is the man who will succeed best in life.

It is by this philosophy one creates his own atmosphere and makes his life yield its best and rarest fruits. Every vocation in life implies service. Those who are aspiring to high positions should seek to become the servant of all. So let us come to the rescue of the people and seek to introduce new methods, by which they can better their condition and thereby become public benefactors.

The talent we possess is for the service of all. The truth we hold is the truth of all mankind. Truth has been the same in all ages and is the common property of all mankind. Human estimates of truth may change, but truth itself is invariable. Truth is the written Word of God. It should be a guiding principle in our lives. It should mold our characters and shape our destinies.

The work of life is placed before us. The best service only can accomplish satisfactorily the duties that now await us.

The men and women whom we delight to honor are those who spent their lives in the service of others. The altruistic spirits buried the thought of themselves in their ambition to benefit others.

"He that is greatest among you shall be your servant," is the language of the Great Teacher. To serve is regarded as a divine privilege as well as a duty by every right-minded man. Do something worthy for mankind, is the cry of the civilized world. Give light to those who are in darkness; sustain the weak and faltering; befriend and aid the poor and needy.

It was the service of the learned men that made Greece renowned for her great knowledge in science, art, and literature. It was the service of George Washington that repelled the forces of England and saved America in her infancy.

The people want men and women as leaders who will improve their condition. If we want the people to serve us, we must first be willing to serve the people.

As we go from these university halls into the battle of life, where our work is to be done and our places among men to be decided, we should go in the spirit of service, with a determination to do all in our power to uplift humanity.

One of the truest friends of humanity today in the secular world is Andrew Carnegie, the great Iron King, who has retired from active business and is now distributing his wealth for the benefit of others through the establishment of circulating libraries and endowments for schools.

Abraham Lincoln, whose praises are sung by millions today, recognized the fact that he could perform a service to four million slaves and his country by issuing the Emancipation

Proclamation. He possessed the moral courage to strike off the shackles of those held in bondage and declared them free.

The founders of this university have rendered an immeasurable service by providing an excellent school in which the colored youth can prepare itself for the great work of life.

We must carry to others the blessings which we have received here. The purpose of education is not personal enjoyment. It is a preparation for the most efficient service. It sends us out to do something for the masses.

The people are looking to us for strength and help. They need our best efforts, our bravest words, our noblest deeds, our tenderest love, and our most helpful sympathy. This is a needy world; outstretched hands may be seen by the thousands asking for aid. It is our duty to relieve human wants. Let us place our standard high, but be willing to do 'the lowest task, the most distasteful labor, be ever helpful and generous, and be ready to lend a helping hand.

W. H. Taft, the President of the United States, has recently taken his oath to serve eighty million people. It is the good and faithful service of the president of this university and his loyal colaborers that has won a reputation for our institution, of which we are justly proud.

It was the valuable service of self-sacrificing trustees given to the educational department of our Church in this State that has opened a fountain of knowledge for the colored youth of my race. Good service is an unfailing guide to success. One of the grandest mottoes in the universities today is, "Better to serve than be served."

There is nothing more reputable to a race or nation than Christian service. So let us not hesitate, but grasp every opportunity that will enable us to do some good for

others. As teachers, teach the people; as merchants, supply
their needs; as doctors, administer to their wants; and as
preachers, proclaim the Gospel of our Lord Jesus Christ.

It makes no difference how circumscribed opportunities
may be, show yourself a friend to those who feel themselves
friendless. Do not sit with idle hands, but take up the
first task that offers itself to do—work in the field, at the
desk, at the washtub, tending to customers behind the coun-
ter, or whatever it might be, and be faithful in the task at
hand.

There is no greatness in material things of themselves.
The greatness is determined by the use of them. When we
go out into the world and offer our service to the people, we
must give to the world something that we feel mankind
needs. Cast your bread upon the waters, and you will find
it many days hence.

The following was my

VALEDICTORY

Trustees: Honorable Bishop and Gentlemen of the Board
of Trustees: We know you have been guarding the material
interests of this university, spent your money, offered your
prayers, pleaded our cause to the public, and denied yourselves for our comfort. We are your debtors, and wherever
our lot is cast, your banner shall not trail in the dust.
Honorable sirs, farewell!

Dear President: To you, in behalf of the graduating class,
I bring our heartfelt thanks for the great care you have
taken of our welfare. We appreciate your kind interest,
your courtesy, and your best wishes for our future success.
You have taught us lessons of morals which will abide with
us throughout life, and in behalf of the graduating class of
1909 I bid you a regretful farewell.

Members of the Faculty: The time has come for us to bid you farewell. You have been given the task of impressing upon our minds the truths that will develop us into useful men and women and of implanting the germ of knowledge in our brains and hearts that will grow to form a successful life. You have instilled the spirit of originality in our lives. You have formed in us the habit of study. You have grieved when we failed to manifest the proper interest. You have faithfully discharged your duties. We tremble as we leave you; for here we relied upon your wisdom and guidance and sought your counsel and assistance, which you were ever able and willing to give. Now we must go forth to battle with life alone. We trust you will not cease to pray for our success. We halt as we say, "Farewell!"

Undergraduates: Today we leave you. We leave the old university in your care; you are to walk these halls and paths after we have wandered away. You will make these halls and this campus ring with cheers of gladness and glee in which our voices have so often mingled. But you will have many little incidents in the classroom and on the campus, such as we have often had. We shall feel lonely when we think of you, but our hearts are still with you, even if we must bid you good-by.

Classmates: We are all standing together for the last time. We have formed an unrivaled friendship, which, I hope, will continue throughout life. We have read to the end of the long chapter of our beloved Payne University. Our farewell must now be spoken. We knew this time would come. In imagination we tried to place it a far way off. We wish we should not have to say good-by, but the time has come and, oh! it seems to be such a strange word to us, who have daily met one another. We are nearer to one

another today than ever before. Now we must ever face
the responsibilities of life. We have no president to rely
upon, no dean to solve our difficult problems in life, no
teachers to direct the course of our thoughts. We must make
our mark or fail. Our path will not be easy all the way;
our service will not be appreciated by all. We shall not
stumble into greatness, nor will it be thrust upon us. If we
would win, we must work, watch, and wait. We may be
criticized, but that should not make us feel dismayed. Vic-
tory will surely come to him who works, watches, and
waits. Wherever you stand, let it always be said, "This is a
worthy representative of Payne University." Let us continue to
pray, study, and perform the duties that will reflect credit upon our home, school, church, and race.

Honorable Bishop, dear Trustees, President, Faculty,
Schoolmates, Friends, and Classmates, I bid you one and all
a tender and a final farewell.

———————————

While I was delivering the above valedictory oration,
the entire audience, from the bishop down, wept, except the
president and myself.

When I had ended my speech, Prof. W. H. Bowen came
forward and delivered the commencement address, after
which Bishop H. B. Parks presented the diplomas. He made
a short speech, of which I have kept a few words to this
day. He cautioned us to beware of three men whom we
would be sure to meet on life's journey: (1) the selfish man,
who thinks only of himself; (2) the complainer, one who
always finds fault; (3) the idler, the lazy man.

He referred to the three different spirits as three different
men—the selfish spirit, the complaining spirit, the idle
spirit. He cautioned and warned us not to tolerate such

spirits; for if we did, we should meet with no success in life.

Having made a permanent note in my heart of what he said, I reached forth and received my diploma from the hands of Bishop Parks.

The class song was then sung, and our friends came forward and presented to us many useful gifts, wearing apparel and the like, and extended their congratulations to us.

Thus ended my school life at Payne University.

"Wait on the Lord, be of good courage, and He shall strengthen thine heart. Wait, I say, on the Lord." (Ps. 27:14).

6

THE FIRST YEARS AFTER GRADUATION

•

All things whatsoever ye shall ask in prayer,
believing, ye shall receive.
MATT. 21:22

•

THE MORNING AFTER MY GRADUATION, JUNE 2, 1909, I LEFT
Selma for my old home in the country at Rosebud and arrived
there late in the afternoon.

Having just finished school, I was young and active and
had an ambition to work for the Lord and my race. I was
ready to serve. I had great enthusiasm to serve my people;
my heart was overwhelmed with compassion for them. This
sympathy for the common people has remained with me
throughout life.

I have told you in a previous part of this little volume that
from childhood I desired to be a schoolteacher. Now the
time had come for me to begin my lifework. This inclination
I began to feel very keenly: "Go where you are most needed,
and do something for the masses."

At that time there were in this part of the country some
very peculiar local laws pertaining to the public schools in
certain districts. One was that if the colored people failed
to have a public school for any one scholastic year, the public
school money would be returned to the county and be given
to the support of the white schools.

Most of the so-called public school teachers were not able
to pass the State examination and secure a State certificate.

On that account there were a number of vacant schools every year in nearly every county. Worse than that, in some counties the colored people had no public school at all, no funds having been appropriated for the training of the colored children.

I resolved to render some service to my race by teaching for them each year in as many of these vacant schools as I could and thus help them retain the small public fund that had been set aside for the colored youth.

On June 5, 1909, I went to a place called Piny Woods and held a school meeting. In this meeting I offered my services to teach a summer school for four months, beginning June 7. To this they all gladly and willingly agreed.

To my surprise, when I returned to open the school on June 7, I met with a very unpleasant experience. Not a child was to be seen, and the door was locked. I could not afford to let this obstacle discourage me, for I realized that as I went on through life, I should see greater discouragements.

I put my books and other belongings on the church steps and went over to the deacon's home to inquire why he had locked the door against me. When I reached the house, his wife told me that he was in the field. I took his little seven-year-old girl along to the place where he was plowing and addressed him kindly, politely, and cheerfully. Then I asked him why he had locked the door and where the key was. At first the deacon seemed to be at his wit's end; he stared at me with a big question mark, as it were, on his face. After a few moments he tried to speak and make excuses, "The people—they—the people, they—"

I said to the deacon kindly: "Brother, give me the church key." This he did at once. I then asked him to give me the little girl for the summer school, as she was too small to do anything on the farm. He answered: "I have no objections."

So with the key in my hand, the little girl at my side, and a prayer in my heart, I hastened back to the little church in which I was to teach the school. When I approached the churchyard, I saw a woman with a little boy leaving the grounds. I called to her: "Wait, lady! Why are you leaving?" She began to mutter: "'Caze de do' are locked, an um gying to care me boy back ham."

"Oh, no," I exclaimed, "don't do that! I have the key. Give me this little boy for the summer school; I shall take good care of him." These soft words won the confidence of the woman at once. She smiled and handed me the little boy's dirty book sack and the bucket, with his dinner in it.

After sweeping the church and dusting the benches, I was ready to begin school. With a plantation song, the Lord's Prayer, and those two little colored children I began my lifework at Piny Woods in a little Baptist church called "Coonslide." Why the people named their church thus I do not know; I can only say that it was due to ignorance of what constitutes a proper church name.

In spite of the small beginning my work in Piny Woods was pleasant and successful. Day after day I prayed for a good school, and the Lord granted me success. The enrollment reached forty-five. The children advanced in their studies and made good progress along secular lines. I taught them the Lord's Prayer and some Bible verses. No one instructed me to do this, but I just reasoned within myself that I would see to it that each one of my charges should learn the Lord's Prayer and some Bible verses.

Besides teaching the school in Piny Woods that year, I did some work for the Methodist Church. I served as the secretary of the Camden District Sunday School Convention. I was re-elected to this office for four consecutive years. I served as Sunday school teacher and also conducted a sort of mission society in the Rosebud Methodist Church, where I was baptized.

We closed the summer school in Piny Woods the last week in September, and without a week's vacation I went right on to open the fall school in Pine Grove, Autauga County, the first Monday in October.

While carrying on my work in Pine Grove, I ever remembered the old way that led me to success, namely, prayer. I prayed daily for the children who were committed to my charge. The Lord sent the increase. The enrollment reached fifty, and the children advanced rapidly, to the perfect satisfaction of all concerned.

The Lord has always given me white friends. There lived near the school a very fine white couple which believed in the education of the colored people, Mr. White Jones and his wife. They assisted me in building a schoolhouse for the colored people in that place. Mrs. Jones would often visit the school and address my literary society. She would also supply this society with suitable pieces, which she would clip from her magazines. She showed herself to be a stanch friend of mine in every way.

I closed the Pine Grove school the latter part of 1910 and resumed the schoolwork in Piny Woods the first Monday in February. That spring the school was a decided success. The enrollment reached something over a hundred—I do not remember the exact number. As I had no assistant teacher, it was a difficult task for me to keep all the pupils interested and see that they made good progress in their studies; but by diligent prayer, careful study, and thorough preparation for each day's work I ended the school term successfully. I made an attempt to build a decent schoolhouse there for the people, but I could not prevail upon them to assist me in my efforts, and so I closed the school on the last day of May.

I was now asked to teach the summer school for my home people at Rosebud. Without a week's vacation I began the school the first Monday in June and taught the next four months. Most of the parents and even many of the children knew me from girlhood and seemed to have the greatest confidence in me and respected me, and they did everything in their power to make it pleasant and agreeable for me.

Besides my schoolwork I did some more church work for the people. I was elected president of the Woman's Home and Foreign Missions Society. I taught school daily, visited different churches, and organized mission societies among the women to raise money for the support of their missions here in America and in Africa.

At the close of the summer school at Rosebud in September I was called to Fulton in Clarke County and began teaching the first Monday in October, 1910. I had not been in Fulton a month when I received two appointments, one from the president of the Connectional Preachers' Aid, an organization in the A. M. E. Church, a kind of insurance, with headquarters at Nashville, Tenn., and the other from the president of the A. M. E. Book Concern, whose headquarters are at Philadelphia.

In the performance of the duties of the above-named appointments I was to fill the office of two of the general officers by proxy. Being ready to serve, I accepted the two appointments, hired a teacher in my place, and took up the new work. I visited the four annual conferences that were held in the State that year at Ensley City, Mobile, Eufaula, and Union Springs. It was through this service rendered the A. M. E. Church that I won a four-year scholarship to Wilberforce University at Wilberforce, Ohio. But because I feared that the cold climate would cause the return of the rheumatism from which I had suffered in my youth, Bishop H. B. Parks advised me not to go to Wilberforce. I followed his advice. Later I returned to Fulton and resumed my work as public school teacher.

Soon after I had taken up my work at Fulton again, I received a big inducement from the headquarters at Nashville, Tennessee, to give up teaching altogether and go to Texas as State Superintendent of the Connectional Preachers' Aid. Before taking a definite step in this matter, I consulted with Bishop Parks. He said to me: "I thought you told me you wanted to be a teacher. Teaching school is a broad field for you to work in." Thus he reminded me of my first desire to take up the calling of teaching school. So I remained with teaching.

When I left Fulton, I went to Mulberry, Autauga County, and taught a four months' school during the spring of 1911. In the summer of that year I taught my home school again. That fall I was elected the lady principal in the Fairview Industrial School at Dothan, Houston County. I went to Dothan and served until that Christmas; but owing to the base deportment of the principal of the school with the girls, I resigned a few days before we closed for the holidays and left for home.

On my way from Dothan to Rosebud I met a gentleman on the train, one R. J. Davis. He asked me to go to Nichburg, Conecuh County, to teach the spring school.

I accepted this call, and immediately after the holidays I went to Nichburg and began my work in that school. It was here that I conceived the idea of building a school concerning which you will read in another part of this volume.

I believe in a thorough preparation for teaching. While I was doing all this church and public school work, I was steadily trying to prepare myself for more efficient service by taking a correspondence course. I reviewed all my high school and normal subjects, and for my own benefit I thought I would take the State examination once or twice every year. Thus, in the course of several years, I passed the third-grade State examination seven times and the second-grade State examination four times.

All glory and honor for what I accomplished in those first few years after graduation I give to Jesus; for it was His guiding hand that gave me strength to do all this work of teaching one school after another without a month's vacation. He had taken me through several years of schooling at Payne University, where I obtained a fair secular education, and now He was enabling and allowing me to go from place to place and do this work in order to secure experience in dealing with people, to gain their confidence, and to obtain a broader knowledge of their condition and their needs, with the object in view of using the talent which He had given me to work for His kingdom and of carrying out His command: "Go, work in My vineyard."

All the time my great ambition was to start a school for the people who needed it most.

7

WHY I WANTED TO BUILD A SCHOOL

•

For, behold, the darkness shall cover the earth
and gross darkness the people.
Is. 60:2

•

IT WAS NOT THE THOUGHT OF MONEY THAT CONVINCED ME that I ought to start a school. From the time I received my diploma and went forth from the university into the battle of life, it had ever been my desire to serve. I was ready to serve under any and all conditions. My highest ambition is still to serve, to be a faithful servant of God and my people. I would rather serve than be served. I have never desired a high position. I would rather do the humble work among the despised and outcast. As I saw the great need of my people, my desire to do something for their education grew. And so I might state my reasons for wanting to start a school as follows:

1. I saw the grievous condition of my race, of my brothers and sisters. It was a pathetic sight. The ignorance and the superstition in all matters were amazing. I hoped that my school would help to overcome some of this ignorance and superstition.

2. Morals and manners were at a low ebb. It was a rare thing to see a man who did not have two or more wives or to see a woman who had only one husband. It was a common thing to see a young girl approaching the age of twenty, who was a mother and was drifting about with no husband. Both young and old had lost all regard for the holy estate

of matrimony. There were hundreds of people who had been married, but were separated. It was a common thing to see girls or women living by themselves in little huts dotted over the plantations. Young girls would often bundle their clothes, move out from their father's home, away from the care and protection of a loving mother, and start keeping house by themselves.

The reputation of some of these people was shameful. Their manners in all places, at home, in church, on the roadsides, in public places, such as stores and railroad stations, were rough, uncouth, boisterous. Even their word of honor was of no account. I hoped that my school would help to improve morals and manners.

3. The homes in which these poor people lived were horrible. In every community there were two classes of people, the Big Dogs and the Little Dogs. Of course, in the homes of the so-called Big Dogs conditions were a little more decent. In the homes of the so-called Little Dogs, conditions, upon the whole, were indecent. There were no arrangements made for bathing or ventilation in the houses. In most of them there was too much ventilation. While sitting in the house behind closed doors, one could look up and see the sky, the moon, and the stars through the holes in the roof; one could look down and through the holes in the floor see the ground—chickens, hogs, little pigs, and dogs. One could seldom find a decent pair of steps at a door. The chimneys, made of sticks daubed with red mud reached only halfway up the houses. On a cold day it might happen that the wind would blow down the chimney and that the smoke would prevent the family from having a fire.

In many cases the whole family, half-grown young men and women, smaller children, and father and mother, had to sleep and cook in the same room. The bedclothes were filthy; most of the members of the family would sleep in the clothes they had worn during the day. The dishes and cooking utensils remained unwashed from meal to meal, day after day. The bedclothes, dishes, and cooking utensils were covered with swarms of flies. Scarcely any lamps could be found in the homes, and in most cases where there were lamps they had no chimneys.

There were no dinner tables on which to serve when the dinner was prepared. The mother gave each member of the family his or her dinner on a plate, or in a pan, bucket, or skillet. Some would sit in the doorway, some on the steps, others out in the yard, and the little children on the floor. All ate with their hands and fingers.

Lunch at School

They used gourds for dippers, broom sage and pine tops for brooms. A few chairs, boxes, blocks or wagon-body seats on the floor were used for seats. The floors were seldom, if ever, scrubbed and not often swept. About the yard lay all kinds of filthy rags, inviting disease. Through my school I hoped to improve these conditions by inspiring children and young people to improve also their material surroundings.

4. The children, the dear little children of the rural districts whom I love so well and in whom I am so interested, were in a sad condition. Some of them had to come to school partly dressed in adults' clothing. In the dead of winter some of them would have to come to my school with only one or two pieces of clothing on as a protection against the stings and howls of the winter winds, half hungry, half naked, bare-footed, toes and heels cracked open

from the rain, ice, and frost. Their heads looked horrible. The little girls' hair was combed only once in a while. It was knotty, kinky, dirty, matted, and full of cockleburs. The boys, poor things, their hair was never combed. Once in a while some member of the family would take a pair of scissors and cut the boys' hair, which was so gummy and matted that it would come off in a caplike form. In many cases there were hog lice in the little boys' hair. On their hands, wrists, forearms, in the back of their necks, on their kneecaps, on the front part of their legs, on their ankles, heels, feet, and toes grew banks of dirt until it formed a scaly crust, so thick that you could take a pin and stick deep or scrape hard, and they would not feel it. The finger and toe nails were long and dirty. Their teeth were yellow with stain. The best they knew to do was to steal, lie, curse, swear, and fight like cats and dogs. My heart went out to these children, and I desired to do for them whatever lay in my power to do.

5. The educational advantages offered these children by the State were entirely inadequate. The school terms lasted only three or four months a year. Before the children could get a good start in school, the term would be over. During the long vacation of eight or nine months the children would forget most, if not all, of what they had learned during the previous term. I planned a school that would provide an adequate school term.

6. Among these poor children there were some bright boys and girls, filled with high ambitions, with the marks of leadership on their dusky brows, which shone like diamonds in a coal bed in the bright sun. Their poor parents were unable to send them to school. They had nothing with which to pay their board; they were just barely existing themselves,

However, most of the children were dull and backward. There were large boys and girls said to be in the fifth, sixth, and seventh grades who could not read through a paragraph correctly. If they were asked to spell a simple word, for instance, the word "smooth," they might begin to spell it with a *p* or a *q*. There were large children who could not write the letters of the alphabet or do primary work in arithmetic. They would not have the slightest idea of how to solve the simplest problem. Some ten- and fifteen-year-old boys and girls could not read the first lesson on the chart or in the primer.

I wanted to help all children, but especially to give the brighter and more ambitious ones a better chance in life.

7. As a general thing, there were no schoolhouses; for the most part the public schools were taught in the churches. Most of the churches were dilapidated and so exposed to the elements that one might as well teach outdoors under an oak tree. There were big holes in the roofs and in the floors. Many a time during a heavy shower of rain the large children would have to hold an umbrella over me while I heard a class recite.

In some of those churches there were small heaters, but no flues; so we had to take out a window pane and run the stovepipe out through the side of the wall. When the wind was high on a cold day, the smoke would turn us all away from the fire. In churches where there were no heaters we were obliged to build big fires outdoors. Then I would have to watch the little fellows to prevent their clothes from catching fire.

I hoped to provide a good school in a decent building.

8. The poor people were lacking in leadership. It is one of the great needs of the colored race even to this day to

have sufficient and efficient leaders. The number of able, prepared leaders is so small that real work is difficult.

The public school teachers were inefficient. Not more than one third of them could pass a third-grade State examination fairly well. Some of them did not have the least idea of how to grade a school. They would permit children to enter the sixth and seventh grades that should have been in the third. Discipline in the school was unknown. Before one reached the school building or church where the school was being held, one could hear the children giggling, murmuring, and shuffling their feet. There was a continual commotion during the school hours. The teachers would ask the children questions about their lessons and have to look in the book to see if the child answered correctly.

These teachers would permit the children to sing all kinds of songs and give some of the most ridiculous recitations. The public school teachers would sometimes have Christmas trees and present Christmas programs for the benefit of the community. The following are some of the recitations the children would recite. A little ashy-faced country lad comes forward, so happy that he has a chance to speak that his face is wreathed in smiles. He recites as follows:

> Black gum bits and bullet rains,
> White oak saddle and hickory horse,
> Um gwine to ride all up and down the line.

At this all the people would whoop, shout, and laugh. Then another child would come forward and give his Christmas selection:

> Milk in the pitcher and butter in the bowl;
> I cannot get a sweetheart to save my soul.

Then another would step forward and recite:

> With a jug of molasses and a pan of biscuits in my hand,
> I'll sop my way to the Promised Land.

Now, such recitations were given on the solemn occasion of the commemoration of the birth of Jesus, the Savior of the world. "Gross darkness covered the people."

The so-called preachers often were worse than those to whom they preached. Some were both ignorant and immoral. The better class of laymen would not trust them in their homes during their absence. These so-called preachers were the downfall of many poor, ignorant, young girls. They destroyed the peace and harmony in many a humble country home.

It was a common thing to see a preacher at one of those annual meetings just out of the pulpit staggering down some dark alley, drunk with wine, beer, "shinny," or whisky, heaving like a dog, while the other preachers looked upon it as a joke. Besides this, many preachers were greedy for money. They would rove the rural districts, holding out false inducements to the poor, ignorant people, enticing them to join all kinds of fraternal societies. They would offer the people sick, accident, and death benefits, and every other kind of benefit, just to get their money. Most people could not resist the temptation. Those who had credit would go to their landlords and borrow the money to join. Others would sell their corn, eggs, pigs, chickens, the very food out of the mouths of their little children, to obtain money with which to join these societies. After they had stripped the people of all the money they could get, these scoundrels would escape and no more would be heard from them, while the people were left in need as before.

They would impose heavy taxation, or assessment, upon the church people; and if those who were thus taxed failed to pay, they were excommunicated, or their names were put on the dead list. A person whose name was on the dead list was not permitted to partake of the Lord's Supper. If he became sick, no pastor visited him; and if he died, no pastor would bury him or preach the funeral sermon. Some of these preachers would hire out to the people to preach so many sermons a year or month for so much money. Visiting the sick and burying the dead was not included. A Baptism was performed for twenty-five cents and up per head. When a member died, the funeral was used as an occasion to draw a large crowd in order to get a lot of money.

These preachers would not humble themselves, or feel enough interest in the people, to live in the parsonages the people had provided for them. The homes these poor people had strained themselves to build for them they allowed to go to ruin. The preachers went to the cities, hanging around the streets in the towns during the week. On Saturdays they would go out to their country churches, do their kind of preaching, get all the money, chickens, and eggs they could get from the people and on Monday mornings board the train for the city with these gifts, joking about the people, calling them "niggers" and saying: "I told them niggers so and so." Instead of trying to enlighten the people, they were calling them fools.

My school was intended to contribute its part in developing intelligent and unselfish leaders for my people.

9. I always believed in the education of the heart; for a bright head with a wicked heart stands for naught. It only tends to breed trouble. I knew something was wrong with the kind of religion my people had, but I did not know what was wrong about it. I desired a better Christian training for myself and my people, but I did not know where to find it. The religion of my people was a mere

pretense, a kind of manufactured religion. Those who belonged to church were no better than those who did not. In most of the homes the so-called Christian families as well as the unbelievers lived in envy, strife, malice, prejudice, bitter hatred, yea, hellish riot; in covetousness; in adultery and fornication; in theft and lying.

In hundreds of homes the Bible was never read, a prayer was never spoken, and a Christian hymn was never sung. The whole family lay down at night and rose the next morning, and each went out to do his work without saying a word of thanks to God. Sin was looked upon by most people as a small thing. They held divine services in their churches twelve times a year, on the average once a month. No one took the time to teach them Christian hymns; they sang old plantation songs during their services.

Both men and women would get down on their knees and pray just as loud as they could hollo, often using all kinds of profane language and blasphemy. They would call on God as if He were asleep or dead. The preachers would read a text and then branch off and preach all kinds of man-made doctrines, telling the people that these things are in the Bible. Many a time the name of Jesus was not mentioned during a whole sermon. The preachers would whoop, hollo, pat, and stamp, snort, and blow until the people were in an uproar, shouting and holloing, too. Then the preachers would just say anything. I once heard a preacher laughing and telling how he curses when he gets "niggers" to shouting and holloing.

The people were obliged to carry on most of the church work without the preachers; they just came and preached. The people would have Sunday school about three months out of the year, beginning a few Sundays before Easter each

year and continuing until July or August. They had the
wrong conception of Christmas and other Christian festivals.
I hoped to be of some help in improving the sad religious
conditions, though I did not know just how that might be
accomplished.

10. Though the teaching of the Bible and of the Six Chief
Parts of the Christian religion was neglected, I cannot say
that this was one of my reasons for wanting to build a school
for my race, for in this respect I was in the dark myself. Sad!
Sad! We were all blind and leaders of the blind. We did not
know the Bible, neither did the preachers know it. We did
not know what we must do to be saved, neither did the
preachers. They were preaching false doctrine, and we did
not know it. We did not know that Jesus has done all that
is necessary for our salvation, and the preachers did not know
it. We did not know what Jesus, the Savior, meant to us.
We did not know that we were sinners. We wanted to go to
heaven; but we did not know the way, and the preachers
did not know it. We were trying to work our way to heaven,
and the preachers were doing the same. We were not following our Bibles, neither were the preachers.

Now, what was to be done? Our white people had given
us our schools and churches. We sent calls and had our
leaders; and I presume the white people thought we were
getting along fine.

The Lord, our Savior, who loved us saw all this and
had compassion on us. He saw that the sad plight of our
immortal souls was far worse than our physical condition. The Lord looked down from heaven upon us. He saw
this hellward-leading teaching, this man-made doctrine of
salvation by works. He saw darkness had covered our land.
Our eyes were blind to the knowledge contained in His

blessed Gospel. The Lord saw that we were all on the wrong road, regardless of how well we meant, and could never reach heaven that way.

God saw that I was concerned, that I was worried, about many things pertaining to the temporal welfare of my people. God saw my eager desires and longings to do something for Him and my race. I did not have the least idea of what was to be done. I could not preach, for women are not allowed to preach. But the Lord instilled in me the thought of building a school, gave me strength to begin this work, and sustained me.

At that time I knew nothing about the Lutheran Church and its pure Gospel preaching; but God knew all about it and was pleased with it. God was going to use my school as an instrument to put the true Church in this dark land. The Lord did send us the light through the Lutheran Church, of which you will read later.

8

HOW I BEGAN THE WORK AT ROSEBUD

•

*I will instruct thee and teach thee in the way which thou shalt
go. I will guide thee with Mine eye.*
Ps. 32:8

•

ONE DAY AT RECESS, A FEW WEEKS BEFORE I CLOSED THE
school at Nichburg, Conecuh County, in the spring of 1912,
I was out in the yard watching the poor little half-clad
children playing baseball. While looking on, I seated myself
beside the root of a large old field pine tree in the school-
yard which the children had whitewashed several feet up with
a kind of soil they called soapstone.

While sitting there, my mind wandered back to the many
sad scenes I had witnessed in various sections of the rural
districts during the past few years of service among my
race. As I sat there, the thought came to my mind to
build a large school in the country which would give the
children a longer school term; to run the school on a
cheap basis that would enable the poorest boys and girls
endowed with bright intellects, but not able to defray their
expenses in other schools, to obtain a higher education; to
establish a school that would give the youth a real, true,
threefold education: of the head, the hand, and the heart.

That evening when I returned to my boarding place,
seated by the fire and gazing into the red coals of the
fireplace, I talked to God in my heart a long time over
the school proposition. When I retired, I prayed myself to
sleep over it.

After a few days had passed, I spoke of it to the people with whom I boarded. The news that Miss Rosa was going to build a high school soon spread abroad throughout the community. I had several meetings with the Nichburg school patrons, and we discussed the matter thoroughly; but I did not give them a definite answer in regard to the location of the school. I was undecided as to whether or not Nichburg was the proper place for such a school, as it was located so far from the railroad.

Day after day passed by, and I kept on trying to think of the best place to locate the planned school. I thought I would write and consult my parents about it. This I did at once. I wrote my father that I was going to build a school somewhere in the rural district, but that I had not decided on the location as yet. During the course of a conversation with one Mr. S. E. Ramsey, who lived in Rosebud at that time, my father told him about the letter he had received from me.

Mr. Ramsey told father to write me that I should come home and build the school at Rosebud; the people at home would do just as much for my school as people elsewhere. My father sent me this message. Somehow I readily accepted Mr. Ramsey's invitation and concluded to build the school at Rosebud, my native place. Soon after this I closed the spring school at Nichburg, packed my trunk, bade the good people farewell, and returned to my home at Rosebud.

The first day at home I talked over the school matter with my parents. The next day I sent for Mr. Ramsey. He came to see me that evening, and we had a heart-to-heart talk over the school proposition. Mr. Ramsey pledged his word of honor to stand by me in my undertaking. We decided to hold a school meeting the following Sunday after Sunday school, when I was to present my proposition to the public. I appointed Mr. Ramsey as a committee of one to notify the people of the meeting and to invite them all to come. Mr. Ramsey was a good and faithful man, true to his friends, and reliable in all his business transactions with me.

After this conference with Brother Ramsey I decided that it was necessary to secure the good will and approval of all the white people in the community before presenting my proposition to the colored people, for I said to myself: "This is the white people's country." There was Mr. J. Lee Bonner, the leading white man in Rosebud, who later became widely known in our Lutheran Church in Alabama. Mr. Bonner and his family, of whom you will read more as we continue with this story, were exceptional white people, refined and well educated, sincere Christians, who believe in a Christian education for all.

With a prayer in my heart, I seated myself at the table, uncovered my typewriter, and commenced writing a letter to Mr. Bonner. I began this letter on Monday night after Ramsey had gone. It took me until Friday to complete it. I wished to make every point pertaining to my school proposition perfectly clear, in order to gain the good will and approval of this distinguished family, which meant so much to my work. So day after day, night after night, I prayed, wrote, and rewrote. There was no one to guide, instruct, or teach me just what to say except the Lord. The Lord tells us in His Word: "I will instruct thee, I will teach thee." It was the Lord who endowed me with sufficient knowledge and wisdom to compose this letter. I prayed and struggled over my letter until at last on that Friday night I completed it to my satisfaction. The next morning

I read over the letter, sealed it, and sent it by my father to Mr. Bonner, at the Bonner store. I remained at home anxiously awaiting Mr. Bonner's reply.

The Lord was surely in the plan; for my father says that Mr. Bonner received the letter kindly and read it over four or five times before he said anything. Then he looked up and said: "Tell Miss Rosa for me that if she can do anything to help her race, she can have not only my approval, but also my money." As he continued speaking, his face flushed with excitement: "Your race, the colored people, is an outcast, despised, and downtrodden race." Papa says that he talked to this effect until the tears came to his eyes. God bless Mr. Bonner and his family!

When I heard all this, my heart leaped for joy. I knew the Lord was in the plan. Stealing away from the rest of the family, I bowed down in prayer behind a big tree in gratitude to God for giving me such a strong friend among the white race.

The next thing I decided to do was to draw up a course of study and to devise plans to raise money for buying the land, erecting the school building, and supporting the school, as there were no funds appropriated for such a school. Now, this was the Saturday night before the appointed school meeting, and it took me the greater part of that Saturday night to work out a course of study and devise my plans. I had no one to assist me, not a single individual, no board or organization to consult for advice or suggestions, no board to whom I could submit my resolution for inspection, approval, or adoption. Now, what was I to do? To whom could I apply but to God for instruction and guidance? I sat by the table, bent over my machine, thinking, thinking, thinking, until at last I decided to found my school on the Word of God. Now, it was the Lord who implanted that thought and desire in my heart, for at that time I was in darkness and blind to the truth that leads to salvation as revealed in the Bible.

I adopted the course of study that had been prescribed by the Board of Education for the public schools of Alabama, including such subjects as reading, writing, spelling, language, history, geography, arithmetic, physiology, hygiene; but in addition to these secular branches I resolved to have the Bible taught in my school. For a motto for my school I chose the Bible passage: "Seek ye first the Kingdom of God and His righteousness, and all these things shall be added unto you" (Matt. 6:33). All students were to memorize the school motto. I chose a prayer for my school, the Lord's Prayer. All students who attended the school were to learn the Lord's Prayer. In addition to that, all students were to memorize certain portions of the Psalms and other parts of the Bible which the teacher would assign. The school hymns were to be plantation songs, such as they used at Tuskegee Institute, until I could find time to compile a hymnbook. Now, this was all the Lord's doing, for I have lived to see my desire for a Christian education for my people fulfilled, to wit, in the Lutheran Church, which the Lord has sent to Alabama to enlighten us in His Word.

Besides this secular and, as I called it, Bible Training Course, sewing, cooking, and music were to be taught.

Having composed my course of study, I turned my attention to devising plans for raising money to buy the land and build. The first step I took was to pledge to give up all my living, the two hundred dollars I had saved from teaching in the public school. I resolved to raise the rest of the money by subscriptions from my white friends. Then

I considered ways and means of securing funds for the support of the school after its organization and establishment.

1. I resolved to see the county board of education and the district trustees and contract for the public school fund, which was seventy-five dollars for four months. This was to help pay the teachers' salaries.

2. I resolved to organize a local board of trustees and ask the trustees to pay five dollars a year tuition for their children. This money was also to help support the teachers.

3. I resolved to charge each child one dollar to enter and twenty-five cents a month for tuition. The money thus realized was also to be used to help pay the salaries of the teachers.

On Sunday, after the close of the Sunday school, we held our meeting in the Rosebud Methodist church. There was quite a large number of interested persons, for Brother Ramsey had been busy in the performance of his duty as a committee of one to notify the people of the meeting and invite them to come.

There was no organization; therefore I was obliged to preside. It was not a pleasant thing for a young girl to preside over a body of men, in fact, it was somewhat embarrassing to me.

After the meeting had been opened with a song and a prayer, I arose and read my resolution, including the course of study and plans for securing funds. After much discussion by both men and women, the resolution was accepted. Then we organized our local board of trustees. It consisted of eighteen members.

Thus, on July 8, 1912, was organized the Rosebud Literary and Industrial School. The Lord Jesus, who knows all things, knew the thoughts of my heart and that I meant well. He beheld my desire and longing to do something for the Lord and my race.

Jesus took my little course of study, shabby as it was, together with my plans, and fulfilled them to the letter through the Lutheran Church, which it pleased Him to send down into the Black Belt. We not only have a Bible Training Department, as I called it when I started, but we have wholly religious, Christian schools and churches, Sunday schools and Christian instruction meetings, where the Word of God is taught in its purity and truth, as you will see in reading on.

9

RAISING FUNDS FOR THE FIRST
SCHOOLHOUSE AT ROSEBUD

•

*And all things whatsoever ye shall ask in prayer,
believing, ye shall receive.*
MATT 21:22

•

WHEN I ORGANIZED THE SCHOOL AT ROSEBUD, JULY 8, 1912,
the colored people had no money to give toward defraying
the expense of building a school; therefore I assumed the
responsibility of raising the required capital by soliciting from
the generous public for the cause and of having everything
in readiness for the opening of school on the first Monday in
October, 1912.

The local board pledged themselves to do all they could.
I had no time to lose. Every day had to count, for I had
only three months in which to erect the building, and no
money except my two hundred dollars. That night when I
returned home I prayed over the matter. The next morning
I took the course of study and my subscription list and
went to see Mr. Bonner. As I walked along the wayside,
I talked to God in fervent prayer, asking Him to help me
to raise the necessary funds.

Arriving at Mr. Bonner's residence, I went to the back
steps and waited for someone to come out. The first person I saw that morning was Aunt Jane Ramsey, the cook, a
half sister of my mother. "Aunt Jane," said I, "I want to
see Capt'n." We all called Mr. Bonner Capt'n.

Aunt Jane went into the house, and Mrs. Bonner came out. A glance at her face told me that her heart was with me in my undertaking. She looked at me and smiled, saying, "How are you, Rosa? You came to see the Capt'n?" I answered, "Yes, ma'am."

"About your big school?"

"Yes, ma'am," was again my reply. Then she proceeded to question me about the school. I handed her the course of study. She read it over carefully and remarked, "Rosa, this is nice. Lee told me about the letter which you sent him Saturday and said that he was going to give you ten dollars when you are ready."

Just then Mr. Bonner came into the house. She called to him, "Lee, here is Rosa. She wants to see you about her big school."

"All right," he replied; "I hope she will see me quick, as I must go to the field." After making a few brief remarks, I handed him the course of study. He looked it over and said: "You ought to have a list and take it around and see how much help you can get." I handed him my subscription list. He looked it over, then took his pencil and signed $50, instead of the ten dollars he had told Mrs. Bonner he was going to give.

I could hardly believe my own eyes when I saw him write $50. Returning the list to me, he remarked in a moderate tone of voice, "You may take this to all the white people and see what you can get. There will be no harm in it." I thanked him sincerely and started out on my canvassing tour.

I next went to Mr. J. C. Harper, who had partly raised me from childhood. Mr. Harper had a livestock farm near Neenah, but he resided at Oak Hill. I knew Mr. Harper

was at his farm, so I went to Neenah. As I approached
one of Mr. Harper's pastures, I saw him a great distance
from the highway, having some cattle fed. Making my
way through brush and briars, mudholes and little ponds of
water, I finally reached Mr. Harper. As I approached him,
I said, "Good morning, Capt'n." Looking up in surprise,
he exclaimed: "Why, how are you, Rosa?"

"Capt'n," said I, holding out my papers to him, "I have
a little business matter which I should like for you to look
over if you have time and help me out with it if you can
see your way clear."

He stopped his work at once, brushed his hands, and
reached for the papers. He read them over and smiled,
saying: "Look here, Rosa; Mr. Bonner has given a mighty
heap. What kind of a trade have you made?" I laughed
and answered, "No kind." Then he took his pencil and
pledged ten dollars, saying: "Rosa, I will help you build
any kind of school you want to build." I thanked him and
returned home in prayer, praising and thanking God.

The next day I hitched father's mule to the buggy and
drove over to Oak Hill. As I drove along the road alone, I
prayed almost incessantly, asking the Lord to be with me, as
I was then going among strangers. The first man I approached in Oak Hill was Mr. John T. Dale. I did not
know him personally, but wished to see him first, as I had
heard that he was one of the leading men in the State.
Walking into his store, I said to a colored man standing
near ·by: "Which one is Mr. John Dale?" The man pointed
toward a little office in the rear of the store and said, "He
ìs back there."

I walked slowly back to the office, halting as I came to
the threshold of the office door, and said, "Good morning,

sir." He answered my greeting kindly. I then said, "Is this Mr. John Dale?" He replied, "Yes."

I then proceeded, "Mr. Dale, this is Rosa Young."

"Well, Rosa Young," said he, "I am glad to meet you. What can I do for you?"

"Mr. Dale," said I, "I do not know whether you take any interest in anything like this or not, but I want to get you to look over this little matter and help me if you see your way clear."

He took the papers, and as he read, I watched his countenance change, while his eyes danced from side to side of the page. Then he said: "Girl, you are going to build that school; I want you to build it." He then wrote his pledge and said, "I am going to help you some more."

He did help me from that time on. Mr. John Dale became one of the strong supporters of my work in word and deed. Later he became a stanch friend of our Lutheran Mission and was one of the great instruments in the hands of God in saving our Lutheran Mission in the Black Belt during the War.

The next place I visited was the home of the white preacher of Oak Hill. I approached the front gate and knocked. A kind-looking white lady came out. I said, "Good morning, miss." She answered the greeting. Then I said, "I want to see Mr. Henry, please, ma'am." She answered, "All right; come on in."

When I came to the front steps, the lady walked before me until she came to the door of the study, where the preacher was sitting at his desk. "There is Mr. Henry," she said kindly.

Mr. Henry looked up at me, closed his book on his thumb, and rested it upon his knee. "Mr. Henry," said I, "this is Rosa Young from Rosebud." He repeated thoughtfully, "Rosa Young, Rosa Young." "Yes, sir," said I, and I proceeded: "Mr. Henry, I do not know whether you believe in the education of the colored people or not; but I have a little matter which I should like to have you look over and help me with if you can, please."

He reached for my papers, looked them over, and said: "How much do you want me to give?"

"Just any amount that you feel able to give," said I.

"Well, how much do you think that I ought to give?" he rejoined.

"I would rather leave that to you, for anything you give will be cheerfully and thankfully received," I answered.

He smiled and wrote his pledge and returned the papers to me. He suggested that I see Mr. Dale, Mr. Bonner, and Mr. Harper and ask them to serve as an advisory board for me. "I will help you in any way that they help you," he concluded.

I then went to all the leading white citizens of Oak Hill, introducing myself in the same way as I had in approaching Mr. John T. Dale and Mr. Henry.

The Lord was with me; He guided me as I approached the white people in the interest of my school. By the time I had seen all the men, it was approaching evening, and I was obliged to leave for home, as I was alone. I must say that in my past life I have visited a number of small Southern towns, but I have found no town where the average of culture and intelligence is as high as among the white people of Oak Hill; in fact, it is far above the average; it is an exceptional, a model town.

When I returned home that night, I prayed fervently, giving praise and thanks to God for the success He had given me among those leading white people. Not a man to whom I presented my papers had turned them down thus far.

The next trip I made was to Neenah. There I was quite well known, for it was my post office. All those to whom I presented my papers gave me a pledge.

By this time I had just about canvassed Rosebud, Oak Hill, and Neenah, receiving a total of $101.85.

Having this amount of money in sight, I turned my attention to the purchasing of a site on which to erect the school building. The present five-acre plot on which our church at Rosebud is located was originally owned by my grandfather, old Sam Bonner, my mother's father. Once upon a time Grandpa Sam moved from Rosebud to Camden, and lived several years with Mr. W. J. Bonner, one of Mr. J. Lee Bonner's brothers. When Grandpa tired of living in Camden, Mr. Bonner gave him some money and told him to buy himself a little home. Grandpa followed this advice, returned to Rosebud, and purchased these five acres. After the death of Grandpa Sam and Grandma Hannah, the land came into the possession of their heirs, my mother and her two brothers, Ollie and Press Bonner.

I consulted with these three heirs to buy the five-acre plot for the site of my school. After much quizzing on the part of the heirs and pleading on my part, I succeeded in securing the land for the sum of fifty dollars. This money I took from the sum of the two hundred that I had pledged and paid them for it.

When Grandpa Sam purchased that land, he never, I dare say, dreamed that some day a Christian church would be located on the place. Sometimes while I am sitting in our Christ Evangelical Lutheran Mission at Rosebud, listening to the preaching of the pure Gospel, the singing of the hymns with their German melodies, beholding the true administration of the Holy Sacraments, I wonder whether, if Grandpa Sam and Grandma Hannah were just permitted to visit their little lonely cottage nestled behind a clump of pines a little way back from the public highway, they would be able to recognize the site of their former little homestead. God surely works in a mysterious way.

Dear reader, there is such a deep feeling in connection with this plot of land and the coming of the Lutheran Mission into Alabama that it is my will and desire that our mission may ever remain here until it is proclaimed that time shall be no more; and when I depart from this life, no matter where I may be when I am called to yield up my spirit, may my remains be laid away to repose somewhere in our mission churchyard, on this plot, until the day of general resurrection.

Having secured a clear title, I called a meeting of my local school board, to read it to them. To my surprise, instead of receiving congratulations, I met with criticism. I had had the title made out in my name. I realized then that these poor people would not be able to support a large school, and I thought I would seek a stronger source of support. At that time I did not have the least idea what that source would be, but I firmly believed the Lord would help me to interest some source of help when the time came. I thought I would have no trouble in changing the title of the land; but, on the other hand, if a number of persons were required to give their signature or consent before the title could be changed, it was doubtful whether I could ever get all to agree. But no matter how I explained things, my local board would not hear me. After a heated discussion we decided to send a committee to Mr.

J. Lee Bonner for advice and then adjourned. Capt'n Bonner told them: "That is the thing to do. Let Rosa hold the title; and probably she can succeed in getting some one to help her. We white people all have trusted, and we are willing to trust, her with our money to build a school for the colored people." That settled the affair of the title, and we proceeded.

I then set out to find some lumber for building. In those days, sawmills were few and far between. I went to several different sawmill camps and talked and figured on lumber, but because of the exorbitant prices I could not make a deal. I continued to seek for lumber until my brother Sheffield one day told me about a sawmill that was opposite Pine Apple, a village town a little to the south.

The next day Sheffield and I went to this sawmill and asked for Mr. Arthur Lee. After figuring and figuring we came to an agreement. He promised to let me have the lumber for $20 per thousand. I was to pay down a certain sum and the balance in partial monthly payments.

I returned home and went through the community hunting for wagons. I asked every man in the community who owned a wagon to haul a load of lumber free of charge. The colored men did not have any money to give me for the building, but at my request they started their wagons rolling. For nearly two weeks, mostly at night, one could see wagonloads of lumber and hear the men throwing the lumber on the school ground. It was in midsummer and so hot that the men had to do most of their hauling by night.

After a considerable quantity of lumber was on hand, I started out to find a carpenter. I went to more than half a dozen men and was turned down because I did not have the amount of money they wanted for building the school.

At last I went to "Brother" Nathan T. Ramsey. When I approached him, I said: "Mr. N. T., I have come to get you to help me, and I do not want you to deny me."

He requested me to tell him what it was about. I then explained to him that I had asked so many men to build my school, but that they had all turned me down because I did not have the amount of money they required. "Brother" Ramsey and I continued to talk and figure until at last he agreed to build my school as a deed of charity for $190.

Soon after this, "Brother" Ramsey called his men together and began work. One day, when I came to the building, "Brother" Ramsey had thirteen men hired, paying each a dollar a day. They were to receive their pay that night, and I did not have one penny. I had spent all the money I had solicited, together with the remainder of mine, in buying various materials for the building.

I talked with Ramsey, went home, hooked up the old mule and buggy, and started out for Camden, the county seat, to secure money for paying those men that night. I prayed all the way, asking the Lord to be with me.

When I reached Camden, the first white gentleman I approached in the interest of the school building was Judge Stanford, probate judge. I went up to his front steps, where he was sitting on his porch, introduced myself, and presented my papers together with my usual request. He read the papers and then remarked: "I do not know why everybody who wants something comes to me. Because I am an earthly judge, I suppose." He gave me a donation.

From there I went to a number of the leading men in Camden, not to all, for I wished to return in time to pay

"Brother" Ramsey's day laborers. The Lord was with me. The result of that day's canvassing in Camden was $24.15.

When I reached Rosebud that evening, it was quite dark. I passed by the home of Mr. Jimmy Newberry and left the money with him for "Brother" Ramsey to pay his laborers.

The first Monday in October was drawing near, and the building was not yet finished. I had to begin to make preparations for the opening of school, employing teachers and raising funds wherewith to pay them.

The Lord is wonderful. He works in mysterious ways. We did not have enough money to complete the building and no money with which to buy more material. I advised the carpenters to work up what lumber they had, when they would have to discontinue the work until I could obtain more money.

We then held a meeting to raise funds for the support of the school that fall. All the local trustees paid their five dollars; the children of all others were to pay $1 to enter and a class fee of twenty-five cents a month. I contracted with the County Board of Education for the public school fund of $75. Having thus a good sum of money in view for the support of the teachers, we were about ready to begin; but we had to find a place where to teach until the carpenters had finished working up all the lumber. Our long dream was now about to become a reality.

10

ROSEBUD SCHOOL FROM 1912-1914

•

All things work together for good to them that love God
Rom. 8:28

•

When the time came to open "The Rosebud Literary and Industrial School" on the first Monday of October, 1912, the good Lord brought it to pass, for He has told us in His holy Word: "Commit thy way unto the Lord; trust also in Him; and He shall bring it to pass" (Ps. 37:5). Our school building was not completed; so I opened the school with seven pupils in an old hall where the cattle went for shelter during the night.

The Rosebud School is located near the center of Wilcox County, twelve miles from Camden, the county seat; fifty-four miles from Selma, where our present Alabama Luther College is located, and two miles from the L. & N. Railroad. In this region there was a vast number of colored people, but many of them have since moved away.

I was obliged to teach in the old cattle hall for one month in order to give the carpenters time to work up the lumber they had on hand. I will not say they completed the building, for the building I designed was not really completed until the Lutheran Board for Colored Missions came into possession of the property in 1916. I was kept very busy the first month of school; the enrollment increased daily, and I had to get the necessary school supplies. By the help of the Lord I succeeded in purchasing forty-five long benches from the Methodist church body, five heaters, one large school bell, a sewing machine, and in paying a reasonable amount on a nice piano. I received a gift of 150 Bibles and New Testaments for our Bible Training Department from the American Bible Society at Philadelphia and a nice collection of useful books to begin a school library from Knox Academy, belonging to the Reformed Presbyterian church and school at Selma.

The first Monday of November we were ready to move from the old cattle hall into our new schoolhouse, which nestled on a hill behind a clump of pines. There was no public dedication, but I breathed a prayer in my heart to God as I unlocked the door for the other two teachers and the pupils to march in. I gave the Lord the building with all its contents for the uplift of my race and the spreading of His kingdom, for I realized that without God we could do nothing. The music teacher, Miss Lorene Smith, of Selma, played the piano, and we all marched into the school build- and were seated. We then sang two verses of a hymn, while Miss Smith accompanied the singing on the piano. Then we read a portion of Scripture responsively, as we had enough Bibles on hand, repeated the Lords Prayer, and sang two more verses of another hymn. I then delivered a short informal address, in which I stressed the need of a threefold education, especially that of the heart; for I told them that morning, and still hold to my old proverb: "A bright head with a wicked heart stands for nothing; it tends only to breed trouble."

I also taught them the following little problem, which I have often since illustrated to my pupils:

A life$+$Christ$=$Success.

A life—Christ═Failure, no matter what you can do.

After the address, Miss Smith played a march, and we all passed out of the chapel into the different classrooms for our regular day's lessons.

The school faculty consisted of Miss Lorene Smith, of Selma, who took charge of the cooking, sewing, and music; my sister Viola, who instructed the pupils in the primary grades from the primer through the second grade, while I was to take care of the students from the third grade through the seventh, if there were any. Both Miss Smith and my sister are now deceased.

Our daily schedule was somewhat as follows: The first bell rang each morning at 8.30, the second bell at 9 o'clock. Then all the children formed a long line across the school-yard; and while the music teacher played the march, they passed with accurate step into the chapel for devotion, which were conducted daily.

After devotions came the regular daily lessons, reading and spelling in all the grades, recess at 10.30, then arithmetic in all the grades, and noon recess from 12 to 1 o'clock.

During the first period in the afternoon each teacher conducted a kind of religious service in her own room. We sang the Tuskegee plantation songs, repeated the Lord's Prayer, and memorized Bible verses. The pupils were required to tell the Bible stories in their own words. After this religious instruction, or service, we resumed our daily secular work, and instruction was given in English, geography, history, spelling, writing, and other subjects.

At the close of school in the afternoon the big bell rang, the teacher played the march, and all the pupils returned to the chapel. Here the roll was called, to which each pupil responded with a Bible verse. This was followed by a hymn, the Lord's Prayer, and music, while the children passed out by grades, marching down the long thirty-foot hall into the schoolyard for home.

The religious exercises were something I myself had planned. At that time I knew of no school that held religious exercises. I had a longing to reach the heart of my pupils. I wanted a really Christian school, but had no one to instruct me just how to conduct it, no one to enlighten me in the Scriptures, so that I might impart it to my pupils. I was just feeling my way along, asking the Lord to take my school and make of it a great religious center. This was one of my daily prayers; but I did not have the least idea how it would be done. All good things come from God, even our good desires. God gave me this desire and longing for real Christianity. He was going to use our little school as an instrument to place the Lutheran Church in the Black Belt to lead us out of our spiritual darkness into light.

Besides the religious exercises and the secular branches we had a debating club and literary society, which met on alternate Fridays.

The first year our enrollment reached 155. School children came from all the surrounding communities, Oak Hill, Allenton, Caledonia, Watson Crossing, Nadawah, Jordan, Dulaney, Brazie, Hines, Camden, Olea, Sedan and Coy. A number of people brought children to board, and our home was soon converted into a regular young ladies' villa. I had my grandfather's little log cabin fixed up for a boys' dormitory, and a number of them slept there, but took their meals at our home. The board was only five dollars a month, and they could pay a portion of that in farm products, if they desired. I felt willing to do almost anything, just to help the poor people out with the education of their children.

So many people brought their children to board that I could not accommodate them all. I was obliged to appeal to my friends to help me out.

In order to support our school, we were obliged to give concerts, entertainments, and picnics. On such occasions we often went to the kind white ladies who were our friends, explained our plans, and were presented with nice cakes, baked chickens, and ice cream to sell for our school.

Mr. J. T. Dale dictated a circular letter for me in which we advertised our school. I had the letter printed and had it broadcast through the mails. By some means unknown to me, but probably through some of my friends, some of the circulars even reached the hands of people living in the New England States, and I received a total of $56 from them.

That year our school was in session only six months. It closed the last Thursday and Friday of March, 1913.

When school closed that spring, I went on a money-begging tour for the benefit of our school. I met with some encouragement and some discouragement. I did not approach the white people on this tour as I did when soliciting funds for the building, but went among the leading colored people in Selma, Montgomery, Mobile, and Birmingham. I stood before lawyers, doctors, professors, bankers, businessmen, bishops, and preachers of all denominations and lectured in the different churches whenever I was permitted. Some gave me donations, some kindly turned me away, while others did so harshly, sneering at me and mocking me. One night while in Birmingham, I was lost. I was on the Idlewild streetcar, going from the north to the south side, and alighted from the car at the wrong avenue. I wandered about for more than an hour and began to grow nervous and excited, when, upon looking up, I saw the tower of a church. I went to the church, for I knew the way well from there, as I had gone to that church many a time.

One evening I addressed the Men's Business League. There were more than one hundred men present, and no women besides myself. After my speech, Professor Taylor, who, jointly with a glee club, had traveled in the interest of the Tuskegee Institute for more than thirteen years, took up the donations for me. The gentlemen gave me $15.

Our second school term began on the first Monday of October, 1913. Our enrollment reached 215. Three other teachers besides myself had to be engaged. We were so crowded that we were obliged to build an addition to the school, a larger chapel.

That year our school was in session seven months. It closed the last of April, 1914. Hundreds of people attended the closing exercises. It was reported by a committee appointed to count the people that besides the white people eight hundred colored people were present.

Soon after the close of school I started out on my tour to solicit money to support the school for the coming year and to complete the much-needed chapel.

"All things work together for good to them that love God." God was leading us all along, and the time was drawing near when He was going to place the Lutheran Church in the Black Belt and to lead us out of darkness into light, for He loved us with an everlasting love. He willed that we, too, should be saved. He was not willing that any of us should perish in that gross spiritual darkness which had covered our section. And this humble little school was to be taken over by the Lutheran Church.

II

HOW THE LUTHERAN CHURCH CAME TO ALABAMA

•

What I do thou knowest not now, but thou shalt know hereafter
JOHN 13:7

•

WE CANNOT UNDERSTAND WHY THE LORD TAKES OUR NEAR and dear ones away from us by death, sometimes while they are in the very prime of life. We cannot understand why our dear Lord sometimes lays us low on a bed of sickness and pain when we should like so much to be well, going about working in His vineyard and doing good to our friends and fellow men. We cannot understand why God, who rules the universe, suffers great steamboat disasters, railroad wrecks, ravages of war, various cruelties, oppressions, persecutions, and all other wrongs which are found recorded on the pages of history. But although we cannot understand these things, we have the divine promise that they are sent to us for our good and that we "shall know hereafter." Yes, hereafter! The blessed hereafter! Let us wait patiently for it in faith till the time when we shall know and understand all these things.

Just as slavery, with all its cruelties and inhuman acts, was a great blessing in disguise, so was the invasion of the cotton-destroying Mexican boll weevil in our country in 1914. Just as God often uses nature, creatures, disease, and death as instruments to bring men to Jesus, so He used the little Mexican boll weevil as an instrument to bring the

Lutheran Church into this dark, benighted Black Belt of Alabama to lead us poor sinners out of darkness into light. "Thou knowest not now; but thou shalt know hereafter," says the Savior.

I heard of the invasion of the boll weevil in Texas when I was a child, but the thought never came to me that some day this little insect would cause me and my fellow men to suffer. As time rolled by, the boll weevil moved slowly, but surely toward our section, probably at the rate of sixty miles a year. As the weevils drew nearer, the Government sent out demonstration agents, telling the people that the boll weevil was coming and that they were to prepare and make war on the invaders.

The Mexican boll weevil invaded our country in 1914 and brought with it hard times. The insects practically destroyed the cotton crops, and cotton was the only standard cash crop in our section at that time. Tenants who had been harvesting large cotton crops could hardly harvest as much as a bale; several would have to lump together their small crops in order to make one whole bale of cotton.

The extensive credit system according to which the landlords had been advancing the tenants money, probably since the time of the Emancipation, was then cut off. There was no advancing whatever. All a man received was what he worked for or paid for in cash. If he made a dollar today, he had to live from it tomorrow. The landlords had to rid themselves of the burden of tenants. Each man had to paddle his own canoe.

This discontinuation of the credit system among the tenants created great excitement; for the colored people had never learned the lesson of depending, trusting, and relying wholly upon God, who has the very hair of their heads all numbered, who feeds the ravens and who clothes the grass of the field. Prior to this time most of the tenants depended wholly upon the white landlords to provide clothing, shoes, food, medicine, and other necessities for them. Cotton, King Cotton, was their greatest aim in life. Now that they had to depend upon themselves, they all went about in deep mourning. "What I do thou knowest not now; but thou shalt know hereafter."

In the fall of 1914, when the time came to open our school, things looked very dark. Business was dull, and World War I had broken out. The enrollment in the school fell, and we were obliged to dismiss one of our teachers. The people had but very little cash. We were obliged to accept farm products in payment of tuition. These I had hauled to Camden and sold for what I could get in order to secure money with which to pay our teachers in part. We fell so far behind in paying salaries that our music teacher was compelled to resign at Christmas.

When school closed in spring, 1915, I had only $12.85 with which to pay the salaries. I gave Sister Viola $12.50, and I kept 35 cents for my salary that year. The saddest part of all was that Sister Viola, who had been with me from the beginning in this schoolwork, resigned and accepted a position in the city school at Prattville, at a salary of $60 a month.

After my sister's resignation I went about in meditation and prayer, thinking also about resigning and trying to secure a position in a school paying a big salary; but somehow I could not resign so easily. There was a tie between me and the little colored children of my school. I could not even entertain the thought of turning them out of school, closing the doors, and letting them go back into darkness,

Thirtieth Anniversary Celebration, 1946, Christ Lutheran Church, Rosebud, Alabama. Rev. H. J. Lehman, Pastor

Mount Calvary Lutheran Church, 1946, Maysville, Alabama

The Old Chapel at Maplesville, Alabama

Chapel-School, Rockwest, Alabama

Pilgrim Lutheran Church at Birmingham, Alabama

Concordia Lutheran Church, Montrose, Alabama

Chapel-School at Montrose, Alabama

Altar Cross Lutheran Church, Camden, Alabama
Rev. W. H. Ellwanger, Pastor

Baptism Group, Cross Lutheran Church, Camden, Alabama
December, 1947

*Graduation Class of 1949, Gethsemane Lutheran School,
Hamburg, Alabama*

Christmas Service, Calvary Lutheran Church, Tilden, Alabama

ignorance, and superstition. No, I could not close the doors. Besides, I felt that by closing the school, all the donations that had been given by our kind white friends would be lost and that thereafter they would look upon us as people who start things, but never finish them.

Thus, not willing to give up the school, I called together our local board of trustees. At this meeting we all agreed to offer the school to the African Methodist Episcopal Church, as we were all members of that branch of the Methodists at that time. This body was to hold an educational meeting in Selma in June (1915). I decided that it was best for me to go to Selma prior to this session, take the matter up with the president of Payne University, and get him to make the recommendation for us, as he had charge of educational affairs.

The worst of all was that I wished to go to Selma and adjust these matters, but did not have my train fare; I had only those thirty-five cents. What did I do? One Saturday evening I took those thirty-five cents, boarded the train, and went to Camden. When I arrived there, I had only ten cents left, and it was nearly sunset, as the train had been late. Where was I to lodge that night? With only a dime I could do nothing. However, I had some relatives who lived about two and a half miles out of Camden. There was nothing left for me to do but to try to reach their home. When I arrived there, they were greatly surprised to see me at that late hour, and all alone. I told them of my mission in Camden.

The next morning, Sunday, I hurried to the parsonage of the Methodist preacher. I showed him my recommendations from Mr. J. Lee Bonner, Mr. J. C. Harper, and the Hon. J. T. Dale. Then I asked the privilege of addressing his congregation in the interest of my school at Rosebud. This he readily granted me. I thanked God in my heart, for I was trying to raise my fare to Selma. Just before the minister closed his service that night, he permitted me to speak to his people. The good people of Camden gave me a nice little collection. I do not remember the amount, but among those who gave were Mr. and Mrs. Ned Allen, who later became charter members of our Lutheran mission at Camden.

On Monday morning I returned to Neenah and went to the post office for my mail. I had a letter from Mrs. Irving, Brooklyn on the Hudson, New York, containing a check for $5. I was very much uplifted in spirit, for now I had more than my fare to Selma.

The very next morning I went to Selma. I had the opportunity of discussing the Rosebud school question with President Archie. He promised to recommend to the A. M. E. Connection in Alabama that it take over the Rosebud school and use it as a branch or feeder for Payne University.

When the board of trustees of Payne University met, Professor Archie kept his promise. Bishop Joshua Jones appointed a committee of seven men to visit the Rosebud school and investigate the matter, but this committee was not to go to Rosebud until he returned from the Presiding Elders' Council in order that he might accompany them.

The Presiding Elders' Council met at Prattville that August. Twenty-six presiding elders from Alabama and Tennessee were present. But God did not will that the Methodist Church should take the Rosebud school, as I see clearly now; for what happened? When the question arose, there was great confusion. It reminded me very much of the story of the Tower of Babel. The men began to fight each other. They fought the bishop, they fought the committee, and they fought over the location of the school. President Archie and Bishop Jones could not prevail. Dean Brooks arose and made this prediction: "If we do not take that school, some other organization will take it. God is not going to let it fall, for that young woman is working too faithfully."

When Bishop Jones saw that nothing could be done, he disbanded the first committee and appointed a new committee of three men, who were to come to Rosebud and deliver to us the message of refusal. Upon the arrival of the committee I held a private meeting with them in the school office. The chairman rose and delivered the message. "Miss Rosa," he said, "there were twenty-six presiding elders present in our council, and they send you greeting. They say that you have acted as a loyal African Methodist. They say you went out since your graduation, built a school, and gave us the first offer. But we are unable to take it. You are now privileged to apply to any other body or association for help in order to save your school."

I answered, "Well, you-all have released me."

"Yes, we have released you," he replied. "Now go and seek help anywhere."

So thus I was honorably discharged; but I felt greatly disappointed. I was thankful, however, that they turned me down so kindly. "What I do thou knowest not now; but thou shalt know hereafter." Thus says the Savior.

Having been denied by the Church of my childhood, I went to seek help from another source. That night I prayed almost incessantly. The next step I took was to appeal to Mr. James T. Dillard of New Orleans, La., the agent of the Anna Jeans Fund. This appeal was denied.

I applied to the agent of the Rosenwald Fund and was denied. I appealed to the authorities of the Slater Fund, but with no success. I cried in vain to the Reformed Presbyterian Church, the United Presbyterian Church, and the American Presbyterian Church.

I then wrote to the mission board of the Congregational Church; but their answer was discouraging. The secretary wrote that they had one hundred colored schools and that if I wished to help my race, he would advise me to close the school and take some other steps, as he thought that the colored people had enough schools. By this time I was almost ready to give up; I was growing weaker and weaker over the matter. "What I do thou knowest not now; but thou shalt know hereafter." Yes, the blessed hereafter!

When the time came to open the school again in October, 1915, the way looked dark indeed. I had met with so many denials and disappointments that I could hardly muster up courage to start. I taught for a few weeks, but I was lonesome and low-spirited. All my assistant teachers had deserted me, and I was left alone with one hundred and fifteen pupils.

At last, one day, I came to the conclusion that I had done just about all that I could do, that I might just as well close the school and write in large print across the door, "Hard times."

Before I did this, I went over to see Mr. and Mrs. J. Lee Bonner, my white friends. I wished to tell Mrs. Bonner of my sad plan, as she had always manifested great interest in my work. That day, when I reached Mrs. Bonner's home, I did not go in to see her immediately, but took a seat under a large oak tree that stood just outside the front yard. While I was sitting there in deep sorrow over the thought of closing my dear school, Mrs. Bonner appeared on her front porch. She saw at a glance the sadness on my face and called out in great surprise, "Rosa, what is the matter?"

I told her of my plan and how I hated to see my school close down.

"Why don't you apply to your Church for help?" she inquired.

I then related the story of the refusal I had met with from my Church. Her face flushed with sympathy, and she sorrowfully said: "Well, Rosa, you have worked hard. I cannot blame you for closing down the school if you have done all that you can do."

We talked a few moments longer, and then I walked slowly away, while she stood within the yard with her arms folded and leaning against the railing of the fence. "Goodby, Rosa," she said; "I hope you will have much success when you leave."

"I thank you, Miss Eula" (Mrs. Bonner's given name), said I.

The next day at school I sat down and wrote Mr. Bonner a letter in which I told him of my sad plan and that the reason I wished to go and seek another position was to make money with which to pay him the honest debt I owed him; for Mr. Bonner had lent me money from time to time to carry on the school. I sealed the letter and sent it to Mr. Bonner's house with one of my schoolboys. That day Mr. Bonner was sick in bed. When Mrs. Bonner told him that he had a letter from Rosa, he opened his eyes and told her to read it. Then he said: "Write and tell Rosa that I know the times are hard and that she, being a woman, is up against circumstances where moneyed men can hardly see their way clear; but if she will stay there and carry on the school, I will cancel the debt she owes me."

When I received these words from Mr. Bonner, I was very much encouraged and felt like going on with my work; but there was a much larger debt pending which I owed Mr. J. C. Harper for hard-earned money which he had lent me to help pay the salaries of my teachers. What was I to do about that debt?

That evening when I left school and was on my way home, I met Mr. Harper riding along the road on his big red horse. I called to him. He halted, and I walked up to him and began to relate my sad plan. As I talked, he remained seated on his horse, holding the bridle reins and looking directly down upon the ground. When I had finished speaking, he said: "Rosa, I know the times are hard, but if you will hold on and teach the school a while longer, you may come out better than you think. As far as the money which you owe me is concerned, you may pay me that just any time when you can."

Again my spirit was uplifted.

That night when I returned home, I prayed and prayed and prayed. Then I decided that I would write one more letter, and if no relief came then, I would close the school. Now, that letter was to go to Dr. Booker T. Washington, our great leader. I wrote Dr. Washington that I felt that he had as much as he could look after in the operation of the Tuskegee Institute; all, therefore, that I asked of him was to give me the names of some individual or association in the North that he thought would help me keep my school alive. The next day I mailed my letter, and then I prayed and waited for an answer.

At last one day a letter came from Tuskegee Institute signed by Booker T. Washington himself. In this letter he told me he was unable to help me in the least; but he would advise me to write to the Board of Colored Missions of the Lutheran Church. He said they were doing more for the colored race than any other denomination he knew of. He liked them because of the religious training which they were giving the colored people. He gave me the address of Rev. Christopher F. Drewes, who was then chairman of the Board for Colored Missions.

Under separate cover, Dr. Washington sent me a small pamphlet called the *Negro Yearbook*. In this book could be found the names and addresses of individuals and organizations helping the colored people. He gave me the number of the page in the book where I could find those addresses and said that if I did not succeed with the Lutherans, I might write to the others, as that would do no harm. "What I do thou knowest not now; but thou shalt know hereafter."

I read Dr. Washington's letter over and over, again and again. Then I waited about two weeks before I wrote to any of the parties he had mentioned, and during that time I prayed almost incessantly; many a night I fell asleep praying over the matter. In writing, I took my cue from Acts 1:23-26, where the disciples of Jesus nominated two men to succeed Judas and cast lots for the Lord to show them which of the twain He had chosen for His disciple in the place of Judas. I wrote to every address on that page of the *Yearbook*, and when I had finished and sealed the letters, I said: "Now, whomever the Lord wills or allows to take my school, his heart He will move to do so; and if no one takes it, I shall be satisfied." Among those to whom I wrote was our own Pastor Christopher F. Drewes.

The letter which I addressed to Pastor Drewes follows:

Neenah, Alabama
Oct. 27, 1915

Rev. C. F. Drewes
St. Louis, Missouri
Dear Friend:

I am writing you concerning a school I have organized. I began teaching here in 1912 with seven pupils in an old hall where the cattle went for shelter. Since then I have bought with money collected in the community five acres of land and erected a four-room school house thereon, besides a chapel which we are working on now, bought 45 seats, five heaters, one school bell, one sewing machine, one piano, a nice collection of useful books, and 150 Bibles and New Testaments for our Bible Training Department.

I am writing to see if your conference will take our school under its auspices. If you will take our school under your auspices, we will give you the land, the school building and all of its contents to start with. If you cannot take our school, I beg the privilege to appeal to you to give us a donation to help us finish our new chapel. No matter how little, any amount will be cheerfully and thankfully received.

This school is located near the center of Wilcox County, twelve miles from the county seat of Wilcox County, fifty-four miles from Selma, Alabama, two miles from the L and N Railroad, amid nearly 1,500 colored people. The region is friendly; both white and colored are interested in this school. I hope you will see your way clear to help us.

Yours humbly,

Rosa J. Young

I mailed my letters and went along praying day and night, asking the Lord to move some one's heart to heed our Macedonian cry, "Come over and help us." I believe in prayer; prayer will bring you things that nothing else can.

One day the mail brought me several replies to the letters I had written. To my surprise they were all refusals. My courage fell when I read those letters; still I did not give up praying entirely, as I had not heard from all to whom I had applied. A short time passed, and one day a letter came from the sainted Rev. Nils J. Bakke. Rev. Drewes had sent my letter to him with instructions to investigate the matter. He made no definite promise in his letter, but all through it, as I read it, I could see gleams of hope and encouragement for me in my great struggle. The most interesting parts of his letter were the questions he asked, some of which were as follows:

1. How old are you?
2. To what Church do you belong?
3. In whose name is the title to the land made out?
4. Do you think we can get a Lutheran church in Alabama?

Rev. Bakke advised me to answer his letter at Immanuel Lutheran College, Greensboro, as he was on his way South at that time. I answered Pastor Bakke's letter and his many questions, but received no reply. I waited a while and wrote again and still received no reply. Somehow I could not give up in this case, as I had done in the others. I wrote Rev. Bakke the third letter; like the woman of Tyre and Sidon, I cried out to him. In reply to this letter he wrote that he had gone from Immanuel Lutheran College to Charlotte. Later I learned that he wrote that letter to me while sitting at Pastor John McDavid's writing desk.

In his letter Rev. Bakke stated that although he doubted nothing that I had stated in my letters, he would rather come and investigate the matter for himself, and he would arrive the twenty-first of the month. Rev. Bakke's delay in answering my letters was not neglect, but simply a test of my sincerity.

The first date he gave was inconvenient for me, as I had to go before the Board of Examiners for the State examinations on December 21. I wrote about this to Rev. Bakke and advised him to come January 7, 1916, as it was the custom to hold a larger farmers' conference at the Rosebud school about that time, and he would thus have the opportunity of addressing a great number of people. He wrote a hasty letter in reply, saying that he would change his date and arrive the seventeenth of December (1915), as he wished to go home for the holidays. When I received this letter, I had already informed the local board that Rev. Bakke would be there January 7, 1916. What was I to do now? I sent him a special delivery, asking him to please wait until January 7, as I had already informed the people that he was coming then. I wished to have a great crowd present when he came. To my great surprise on the morning of the seventeenth of December, I received another letter from Rev. Bakke, saying: "I am too close by to turn back. Meet me tonight at Neenah." God was in the plan; so I laughed and said, "Let him come on. I see that he is a businessman."

Rev. Bakke spent the night of the 16th in Selma at a hotel. He told me that some of the boys tried to discourage him and joked about "this man from St. Louis going to Neenah," saying: "There isn't anything at Neenah; even the postmaster goes to Camden with us every night on the train." Not one person in Selma of whom he inquired about Neenah knew where it was or what there was to it.

Nevertheless Rev. Bakke went down to the Louisville and Nashville Railroad station the next morning and boarded the train for Neenah. On the train he had an opportunity to talk with a white gentleman, Mr. Portner, who lived only a few miles from Neenah. He told this man that his business at Neenah was to investigate a matter pertaining to Rosa Young's school. Mr. Portner knew me quite well and knew all about my schoolwork. He said he was glad to hear that this white gentleman was coming to help Rosa Young out with her school.

When the train stopped, Mr. Portner alighted first to see if there was any one to meet Pastor Bakke. Papa was standing on the platform.

"Is that you, Grant?" inquired Mr. Portner.

"Yes, sir," answered my father.

"Well," said Mr. Portner, "there is an old white man on the train who says he is looking for Rosa Young's school."

"I have come to meet him," replied my father.

"All right," answered Mr. Portner, and rushing back to the train, he soon returned with Pastor Bakke's traveling bag and handed it to my father.

Pastor Bakke came limping down from the coach of the train with a crutch under his arm and a walking stick in his hand. A cold, sleeting rain was falling. He wore three coats, a dress coat, an overcoat, and a raincoat. You of my readers who knew him can picture him to your minds as he limped up to my father and introduced himself.

The old Gospel veteran of many a spiritual battle for the Savior was coming at God's command and direction to tell us about Jesus, our Savior, to preach the pure Gospel to the colored people in the Black Belt of Alabama, to lead us out of darkness into light, and to blaze the way for other missionaries. "What I do thou knowest not now, but thou shalt know hereafter."

Rev. Bakke and my father mounted the same old buggy with which I had driven from time to time soliciting funds for the building of my school. Papa took him to Brother Charlie Bythwood's, where he was to spend his first night among the colored people of the Black Belt of Alabama. Our home was crowded with school children. I had paid Mrs. Bythwood one dollar to take care of Rev. Bakke that night.

When my father returned home that night, he told me all about Rev. Bakke's arrival. The next morning I wrote Mr. and Mrs. Bonner of his presence and sent them one of the books he had sent me, *Our Colored Missions, Illustrated.* Mr. Bonner wrote that he would keep Rev. Bakke two nights for me. I then hurried over to Brother Bythwood's, where Rev. Bakke had spent the night, and knocked at the door. He answered, "Come in."

I walked in and said: "Good morning. This is Rosa Young."

He looked me over, then smiled, and said: "Oh, I am so disappointed. I thought I was going to meet a large, large woman who could hardly get along."

We both laughed, and then we began to talk church and school. This was the first conference in the interest of Lutheran mission work on the Alabama field. I then went to notify all the men to come out to the meeting that evening.

That Saturday evening, December 18, 1915, Pastor Bakke held a meeting with our local school board at the Rosebud schoolhouse. When we were assembled, he asked me to lead in singing. I sang the plantation song "Heavy load, heavy load, Um going to lay down this heavy load." Some years after that Pastor Bakke teased me, saying: "Rosa, you sang that you were going to lay down that heavy load, and you laid it right on me."

Pastor Bakke then prayed and asked the men to express themselves. After all had spoken, they signed a resolution to turn the school over to the Lutheran Church. This Rev. Bakke was to report to the Mission Board on returning to St. Louis. He was then taken to Mr. and Mrs. J. Lee Bonner's home, where he was met with the greatest hospitality.

On Sunday morning, December 19, Pastor Bakke held a Lutheran service in the Methodist church. He chose the following for his text: "For ye are bought with a price; therefore glorify God in your body and in your spirit, which are God's" (1 Cor. 6:20).

Now, that was the first time we poor colored people had ever heard the preaching of the pure Gospel; and when Pastor Bakke had finished, he had a convinced audience.

On Monday morning, December 20, Pastor Bakke visited our school and gave the children a religious talk. That night he was brought from Mr. Bonner's home to our house. We had another long talk about church and school that night. Early Tuesday morning he bade us good day and left for his home in St. Louis.

Pastor Bakke was at Rosebud from December 17 to 21, 1915, and when he returned to St. Louis, God moved him to make a favorable report. Having heard Rev. Bakke's report, Director Drewes called a special session of the Mission Board for the afternoon of January 3, 1916, to consider the question of entering the new field. Pastor Drewes said he was reminded of Paul's vision at Troas: "A vision appeared to Paul in the night. There stood a man of Macedonia and prayed him, saying: Come over into Macedonia, and help us. And after he had seen the vision, immediately we endeavored to go into Macedonia, assuredly gathering that the Lord had called us for to preach the Gospel unto them."

That day, January 3, 1916, was a memorable day for our Alabama missions. The Holy Spirit worked wonderfully among the members of the Mission Board. The Board resolved to enter the door of opportunity at once. They instructed Rev. Bakke to return to Alabama and stay there until the work was well organized. They further resolved to retain the writer as a teacher at a salary of $20.00 a month. Thus was my prayer answered.

The coming of the Lutheran Church into Alabama was providential. God only used me and the Rosebud school as instruments to place this Church in the Black Belt and to lead us poor sinners out of spiritual darkness into light. To begin with, I knew nothing about the Lutheran Church and the great mission work it was carrying on among the colored people, and I had only a faint knowledge of Luther and the Reformation; but Jesus, who knows all things, knew all about the Lutheran mission. Jesus is well pleased with the work of the Lutheran Church and willed to take my little Rosebud school and make out of it a Lutheran school, a Christian school, a Bible school for the saving of souls.

God, who is able to do all things, could have used any of the other sources to whom I had so earnestly appealed for help to sustain the school, but He caused every other source to which I applied to refuse me help until I had applied to the right source. It was God who moved the hearts of Director Drewes and the sainted Pastor Bakke to take the steps they did. Yes, it was the hand of God. It was a direct answer to my prayer. Many a day I walked from my home to school, praying every step, asking God to take my school, not to let it die, to make out of it a great religious center. Mrs. J. Lee Bonner also prayed for me and my school. God answered these prayers by sending the Lutheran Church down into the Black Belt to lead us out of darkness into light. "What I do thou knowest not now, but thou shalt know hereafter." Let us always wait for the blessed hereafter.

12

THE BEGINNING OF LUTHERAN MISSION WORK IN ALABAMA

•

Come over into Macedonia and help us
ACTS 16:9

•

THE RECORD OF OUR LUTHERAN MISSION WORK SHOWS THAT Rev. J. F. Doescher, the first missionary sent out by the Board for Colored Missions to explore the Southern States, to preach to the colored people wherever permitted, and to observe their spiritual condition, visited Alabama and organized a Lutheran Sunday school at Mobile. At that time the Mobile station did not look so promising, and for lack of funds and workers it was closed in 1881, nine years before I was born.

For thirty-four years after this station was closed the 900,000 colored people in Alabama did not have the opportunity to hear the preaching of the pure Gospel, which was brought to light again by the sainted Martin Luther, the great Reformer. They lived, and many of them died, with their eyes blinded to the true way of salvation.

Did the God of Love, who gave His only-begotten Son to suffer and die for the sins of all mankind, mean to suffer the 900,000 colored people in Alabama to perish in gross darkness and be eternally lost when He permitted the Mobile station to be closed in 1881? No, that cannot be; for we know "God is not willing that any should perish, but that all should come to repentance." "God so loved the world that He gave His only-begotten Son, that whosoever believeth in Him should not perish, but have everlasting life." God says that whosoever believeth should not perish. That blessed word "whosoever" means the colored people, too. God loved the world, He gave His Son to die for the world, and we, the 900,000 colored people in Alabama, also belong to the world. Therefore God, in His wise providence, out of infinite love for the souls of all mankind, remembered the colored people of Alabama and worked out a plan by which He would give them the golden opportunity to hear the pure Gospel, to believe it and be saved, to be eternally happy in heaven with Him and all the angels of light.

When I wrote that letter of appeal to Pastor Christopher F. Drewes in October, 1915, thirty-four years after the Mobile station had been closed, I did not so much as dream what great blessings would result from it. I did not know Pastor Drewes, I knew nothing about the Honorable Mission Board, nothing about the great mission work that was being carried on among my race by the white Lutheran Christians; in fact, even the name of the Lutheran denomination was unknown in this section among the common people. On the other hand, Pastor Drewes did not know me, the Honorable Mission Board knew nothing about Rosa Young, nothing about the humble little school at Rosebud, nothing of the hard toil I had undergone in order to establish and maintain such a school for the benefit of my race and the spreading of Christ's kingdom. There was no one to introduce or recommend me to them. I dare say that not a single member of the Lutheran faith had ever heard the name Rosa Young. We were all entire strangers to each other. Neither knew anything of the work of the other;

but God knew us. He knows all things. He knew about
my humble work and untiring efforts to do something for
Him and my race. He knew the intents of my mind, its
innermost desires.

God knew the Lutheran Church from of old. He knew
her works, the preaching of the pure Gospel, the true administration of the holy Sacraments, the Christian dayschools,
where His lambs are fed daily, the hymns of praise and
adoration to Jesus which are sung by millions of Lutherans
throughout the world today, and willed to bring me and
my race in touch with the Lutheran Church in order that
we might have the light of the Gospel.

The Holy Spirit worked among the members of the Mission Board wonderfully at that special meeting, January 3,
1916. After they had resolved to enter the new field at once,
Pastor Bakke was instructed to return to Alabama and remain there until the work was well organized. Mr. J. Lee
Bonner and I had suggested to Pastor Bakke that it would
mean much in the work if a good colored man were placed
at the head after it was well organized; therefore the Mission
Board instructed Rev. William Harrison Lane, who was then
a missionary in St. Louis, to come to Rosebud also.

Shortly after this, Pastor Bakke wrote a letter informing
me of the action of the Mission Board. It was on a Sunday
in January, 1916, while I was sitting in the Methodist
church at Rosebud, that Mr. Bonner's cook handed me the
letter from Pastor Bakke. I opened the letter and read it,
holding it down behind the seat in front of me. By the time
I had finished reading it, the Methodist preacher had ended
his sermon and had seated himself. Soon after I arose and
passed out of the church, leaving my twenty-five cents church
dues on the collection table. Since then I have gone to that

*Participants at the Celebration of the 25th Anniversary of the
Founding of Alabama Lutheran College, Selma, Alabama,
November 13, 1947*

*Faculty, Student Body, and Grade School Children
Alabama Lutheran Academy, 1945-1946*

Dedication Service, Boys' Dormitory, Alabama Lutheran Academy, November 5, 1948

Faculty and Graduating Class, 1948, Alabama Lutheran Academy. Front row, left to right: Fred Andrews, Josephine Kent, Eula Mae Coles, Nancy Coles, Lucile Clark, Carrie Jones, Ruth McWilliams, Mary P. Davis. Second row: Rev. P. R. Hunt, Professor S. O. Lacey, Rev. R. F. Jenkins, Rev. R. E. Neely (Commencement speaker), Miss Evie Dale, Rev. A. Dominick, Rev. W. H. Ellwanger, Supt., Miss Rosa J. Young

Alabama Lutheran Academy. College Campus, Selma, Alabama. Grade school extreme left. Chapel and classroom building right of center. Girls' dormitory right

Bible-Story Period, Teacher-Training Class in Children's Literature, Alabama Lutheran College. Standing, Ruth McWilliams, Essie Smith, Students; Mrs. W. H. Ellwanger, Teacher

Aalabama Lutheran Academy, November, 1949. Group Seated in Front of Boys' Dormitory, Dedicated November 5, 1948

church only once, and that was to attend my sister Viola's funeral.

Pastor Bakke arrived in Rosebud to begin mission work on January 13, 1916. Mr. John Bonner, the eldest son of Mr. J. Lee Bonner, met him at the station. Pastor Bakke boarded at the home of the Bonners during his stay in Rosebud. It was a great help for him to live with this reputable family during his work among the colored people, which was a new thing in this section.

Five days after Pastor Bakke's arrival he unfurled the banner of Lutheranism in the Black Belt. He changed the school from a secular school to a Christian school. He organized a Sunday school, a class for Baptism, and a confirmation class. In a heart-to-heart talk with me one day he said, "Rosa, it is a great thing to be a Christian." I did not know what he meant then, but I know now.

Each morning our school opened with short devotions. This was followed by a religious lesson, during which Pastor Bakke would catechize the whole school. Then the children recited verbatim the Bible History stories and the text of Luther's Small Catechism. The advanced pupils recited both text and meaning. After the lesson in religion, Pastor Bakke assisted me in teaching the secular branches until the arrival of Rev. Lane, February 6, after which Pastor Bakke taught religion, Rev. Lane instructed the advanced pupils, and I taught the smaller children.

The first Christian hymns which Pastor Bakke taught us to sing were the following: 1. "My Hope is Built on Nothing Less," 2. "Come, Thou Almighty King," 3. "Let Me be Thine Forever," 4. "I Love Thy Zion, Lord," 5. "Abide, O Dearest Jesus," 6. "Abide with Me, Fast Falls the Eventide," 7. "Alas, and Did My Savior Bleed," 8. "I Know that My Redeemer Lives."

Those words of praise to Jesus and the sweet German melodies made a lasting impression upon my heart. I thought then, and still think to this day, that the Lutheran melodies are the sweetest in the world. Give me my Lutheran melodies. Pastor Bakke had much patience and manifested a world of love for the colored people and a deep interest in their welfare. "Doc," as we affectionately called him, carried the colored people in his bosom. During instruction periods for Baptism and Confirmation he would permit the people to ask questions, and sometimes in the midst of the sermon he would stop to answer a question.

In his audience there were always many who could not read. He would take time and teach them to sing the Lutheran hymns, one line at a time. He continued this method until even the little children and ex-slaves could sing well a few stanzas of certain Lutheran hymns and recite the Lord's Prayer and the Apostle's Creed.

In meeting after meeting the bold and fearless preacher preached Christ and Him Crucified; he defended the Cross; he proclaimed "Luther's doctrine pure" without fear or favor. The people flocked to hear him in great crowds from Rosebud and adjacent communities. Some came seeking the truth, some came to find fault, to criticize, and to condemn, while others came out of mere curiosity to hear this strange religion, as they called it.

The local preachers, having more influence among the common people than Pastor Bakke, went about and poisoned the minds of the so-called churchgoing people against him and prevailed with some of the catechumens to have their names erased from our list. They circulated all kinds of slander and even tried to turn our kind white friends against us. But God used Mr. and Mrs. J. Lee Bonner and the Hon. John T. Dale as instruments to stop such wicked plans. The local school board was broken up. Many who had been strong supporters of our school deserted us and went no farther with us. The Methodists and Baptists united their forces and took a decided stand against Lutheranism.

In spite of the work of these combined forces to stop the work, Pastor Bakke continued to preach the Word, the whole truth. And the Lord added to his list from time to time such as would be saved.

It was in the Christian instruction meetings that I was first convinced of my sins. Pastor Bakke took the Law and showed us our sins and the wrath of God. He showed us what a terrible thing sin is, that we all have sinned, and that, unless we accepted the Savior of sinners, we should all be damned. There were a number of hearers who, like myself, became terrified and alarmed. Then he proclaimed the sweet Gospel-message and showed us our Savior and the grace of God. There was where I first learned to know what my Savior meant to me. There is where I became a Lutheran.

God was working with us. On Palm Sunday, Pastor Bakke and I, who had sown in tears, came forth rejoicing and bringing our sheaves with us, for this was the first confirmation day. When Pastor Bakke was ready to begin the confirmation, he gave me the signal with a slight bow of his head. I drew near with faith, knelt down in the presence of a large number of people, and vowed to be faithful to the Lord and to my dear Lutheran Church unto death. Pastor Bakke placed his hand upon my head and quoted the following Bible-passage: "He which hath begun a good work in you will perform it until the Day of Jesus Christ." Phil. 1,:6. Thus I became a Lutheran and severed my connection with the Methodist Church. I passed to my seat and thanked God that the light had shone into my heart, that my eyes had been opened to the way of salvation, that I was no longer in darkness.

I was the first one to be confirmed in Alabama, and a host of others followed; fifty-eight were baptized, and seventy were confirmed that day. Pastor Bakke said that it was the largest class which he had ever confirmed at any one time.

We had divine service on Good Friday. Pastor Bakke preached Christ and Him Crucified to a packed house. On Easter Sunday he baptized more persons and organized our Christ Congregation, the mother church in Alabama. The new congregation consisted of seventy confirmed members, one hundred baptized members, and twenty-two voting members. After the organization we had our Easter program, the first wholly religious program ever presented in Rosebud.

Pastor Bakke was a tall, majestic figure, even though he was a cripple and had to walk with the aid of a crutch and a cane. In spite of this handicap he made many visits. Saturday was one of his chief visiting days.

"Doc" would walk on Saturday to Lee Bonner's blacksmith shop and stand in the heat of the roaring bellows, talking above the blows of the hammers as he greeted men and told them about Jesus. There he found many names for his Baptism and confirmation classes.

He would often limp to the grist mill and lean against the white dusty walls to talk to the men, women, and children as they came for their sacks of meal, telling them of Jesus and his love for sinners.

From the grist mill he would make his way to the village store, where he had a chance to see practically all the people of the community. There the people often tarried, thus giving the "preacher" just the opportunity he wanted to visit and meet the people.

On week days when he returned from school, he would often take a chair by his window and watch for passers-by, to whom he would wave and beckon to come in for a visit. Then he would take them to the back porch or back yard, for he would not have thought of embarrassing his host or hostess by talking to his colored friends on the front porch.

Mr. J. Lee Bonner had lent Pastor Bakke a horse and buggy to drive to school. One morning a baby colt made its arrival, and Mr. Bonner asked the pastor to stay at home a few days until he could drive the mother horse. The Pastor agreed that the horse should not be driven, but for him to miss his classes was quite another question. As soon as breakfast was over, he took up his cane and crutch and started on the dusty six mile walk. He arrived about 10:30, his face flushing like a live coal and wet with perspiration.

Surely he performed his task as a faithful servant of the Lord, working the works of Him that sent him while it was day. He realized that the night would come when no man could work.

Besides the preaching and teaching during his stay at Rosebud, Pastor Bakke supervised the remodeling of the schoolhouse and the completion of the new chapel we had begun. In order to help me prepare for my work as a mission teacher, he gave me private lessons in religion. Every Saturday morning I went to Mr. Bonner's home and received Christian instruction from nine to eleven o'clock.

While sitting at the feet of Pastor Bakke during those religious periods, I heard wonderful things about that old, old story of Jesus and His great love for sinners. I received rich treasures. I found the pearl of great price, which I will not cast away, if God is with me, for ten thousand worlds.

Having the work well organized, Pastor Bakke returned to St. Louis shortly after Easter. He had been in Rosebud three and a half months. The morning he left, the entire school and a large number of the members met him on the way to the station, waving handkerchiefs and flowers as the car passed by, bidding him good-by. They flocked to the road and to the railroad station to bid farewell to the man who had shown them the way of life. My reader cannot well imagine how lonely this little flock was without their beloved shepherd. Tears flowed freely.

Sad to say, it was not long until the members of the Lutheran Church were mocked, ridiculed, and accused of joining the Lutheran Church for earthly gain. They were called fools who did not know what they were doing. This persecution came from their own relatives, from neighbors, from preachers in other denominations, from teachers, from rude children. If disaster was visited upon the community, people were quick to place the blame on the "Lutherans."

But in spite of all malicious statements, the members remained true to the Savior, whom they had learned to follow. But a little later trouble was to come to them from within their own ranks. A new pastor came, but he was not a faithful shepherd. He had been in the Lutheran Church only a few months. He was unkind to the people, inconsiderate, impatient. The life he lived weakened the whole flock. Some began to think they had made a mistake by leaving another church to come to the Lutheran church.

Some threatened to leave. But God sent a man to comfort and encourage the people, a layman, James McBryde of Detroit, Michigan. In a meeting in which the doubting flock was trying to come to some conclusion, he arose and said: "Men, this man who is here as your pastor is not the Lutheran Church; he is only a member. Let us make up our minds and go forward." From him the people learned to see things differently.

The white friends were greatly interested. They began to inquire of their tenants about the trouble with the newly organized church. By this time I had been transferred to a new field, where we were trying to start a new mission. One day a letter came to me from one of these white friends asking me to write to the Missionary Board to send Pastor Bakke again to Alabama. In this letter he stated that he and all the white people in the community had confidence in this pastor and approved the Lutheran Church.

Pastor Bakke was sent back to Alabama on Sept. 25, 1916, and remained on the field until October 3, 1920. Because of increasing years it seemed unwise for him to remain longer. A great farewell meeting was held at the Oak Hill church. I can never forget that day, nor the words he said as he bade me good-by: "Rosa, I leave you in the hands of God, who created you; I leave you in the hands of God, who redeemed you; I leave you in the hands of God, who sanctified you. And now, if you fall away from the Church and are lost, you cannot say on Judgment Day, 'Lord, I am lost because Pastor Bakke, whom you sent to Alabama, did not tell me the truth,' for I have told you the truth, the whole truth. Good-by, Rosa." He left. I never saw him again. By the grace of God I was the first colored person he had confirmed in the State of Alabama.

He was gone from us scarcely a year until the Lord called him to his reward.

Christ Church, the mother church in the Alabama Field, had 142 baptized members, 62 communicants, 17 voting members, 45 in Sunday school, with $513 in contributions for the year 1946.

13

THE GROWTH OF LUTHERAN MISSION WORK IN ALABAMA

•

Arise, therefore, and get thee down and go with them, doubting nothing; for I have sent them
Acts 10:20

•

IT IS INDEED MARVELOUS HOW THE LORD JESUS PRESENTED opportunities, one after another, so that our Lutheran Church could spread .in the Black Belt of Alabama. Dear reader, let me entreat you to pray as you read this part that you may see the almighty hand of God extending still farther and that the pure Gospel may be preached to all who still grope in darkness.

OAK HILL

The news of the organization of our Lutheran church at Rosebud soon spread abroad in all the adjacent communities. Brother James McBride of Oak Hill heard of this new denomination and its strange doctrine and came to Rosebud to see and hear for himself. That Sunday, while he was sitting in church, listening to Pastor Bakke's voice as he proclaimed the truth, Brother McBride was touched by the Holy Spirit. After the service he came up and joined our catechumen class for confirmation. After his confirmation he returned to his home and would not rest nor hold his peace until a Lutheran church was organized at Oak Hill. St. Paul's Mission was begun there by Rev. Bakke, April 15, 1916. In 1946, St. Paul's numbered 143 baptized members and 35 communicants. 50

127

attended the Sunday school and 30 the Christian day school. Many former members have moved away to other parts of the country and have joined churches there.

POSSUM BEND

One day while I was teaching school at Rosebud, in 1916, an old, dirty, yellow man came up and took his seat under an oak tree in the schoolyard. Rev. Lane threatened to drive him away, as he looked very much like a tramp or a runaway. I begged Rev. Lane not to do that, but to let us find out what he wanted there. Rev. Lane then gave me permission to speak to him. The man's name was Alex Etheridge. To my great surprise he wished us to place a mission at his home in Possum Bend. He had been working at a sawmill at Rosebud, that was why he was so dirty. On the nights that we had meetings he would come and sit in the yard, listening to the preaching. He said he felt too dirty to come into such a nice church. I encouraged him to go home and make a start, which he did. He kept writing me from time to time, until at last God sent His servant Rev. Bakke to Possum Bend; it was Thanksgiving Day, 1916. He organized a mission and called it "Our Savior." Alex Etheridge died in the summer of 1922, during Pastor Marmaduke Nathaniel Carter's administration, in the full triumph of faith in his Savior. In 1946 Possum Bend had 211 baptized members, 105 communicants, 75 in the two-teacher Christian day school, and 70 in the Sunday school.

VREDENBURGH

Sarah and Mary McCants, twin sisters, who were boarding at my house while they were going to school, at the time when Rev. Bakke first came to Alabama, were confirmed in the first class Rev. Bakke had at Rosebud on Palm Sunday, 1916. Shortly after, they went home and made preparations to start a Lutheran Sunday school there. Their old friends and relatives tried hard to induce them to sever their relations with the Lutheran Church; but all their efforts were in vain. Their father gave them an old log cabin about a mile from their home. The girls scrubbed it and made some seats out of old pieces of a wagon body which they carried there from home on their heads. June 1 I received a message from Pastor Bakke to go to Vredenburgh. The next day I took my suitcase, first on my back, then in my hand, and walked the fifteen miles to Vredenburgh. It was very hot and dusty. I was obliged to inquire my way, as I had never gone over those roads before. I often stopped to drink water from the little streams I crossed, to quench my thirst. I arrived there late in the afternoon. That Sunday I named the girls' little Sunday school St. Andrew's.

BUENA VISTA

The mission at Buena Vista was started by one who failed to prove his worth to the congregation, and who finally fell by the wayside. But the church remains with its Christian day school, its Sunday school, and an active band of communicants. I first went to Buena Vista on August 20, 1916, having been invited there by the man who wanted a Lutheran mission. I rode in an oxcart with Sister Luella McCants. That day I did not get a chance to speak to the people; so I remained overnight, but Sister Luella McCants returned with the oxcart that night. The following evening I spoke to a large crowd. Quite a number expressed the desire to have a mission there. After making the second trip, I organized a Lutheran Sunday school and called it St. James's Sunday school.

TINELA

I was sent to Tinela to see Mrs. Cannon, a white lady, for the purpose of buying a plot of land for the new chapel at

Vredenburgh. In order to get a favorable hearing with Mrs. Cannon, I first handed her my recommendation from Mr. J. Lee Bonner. During our conversation I gave her some of our Lutheran literature and explained a portion of Luther's Small Catechism. Mrs. Cannon remarked that she thought it would be very helpful to the colored people of Tinela to hear such teachings. At first I declined, saying that I had not been sent there to do mission work, but to buy land. She smiled, but continued to insist and gave me the names of some colored people whom I should see before I left. I could not resist the temptation; so I called on the parties, and they made a date for me to return and speak to the people.

I returned to Tinela on October 15 and held a meeting in the Union Baptist Church. On the next trip to Tinela, November 12, I held a meeting in a dilapidated house of antebellum days.

Pastor Bakke and Rev. Otho Lynn both made separate trips to Tinela. The impression made upon them was unfavorable; so Rev. Bakke ordered me to go there and take up the Sunday school books. I went to Tinela on the last day of December, 1916. The people were in the old log house, carrying on their Sunday school. They were so glad to see me that at first I hated to tell them that I had come for the books. When I did tell them, they begged that I should give Tinela a chance and not take the books.

I appointed a meeting for the next day at ten o'clock and advised them to bring all the books. We met the next day, January 1, 1917. There was a large crowd. We opened the meeting with a short devotional. I then addressed them and gave them the privilege of speaking for themselves and asking whatever questions they wished. Fate Pryer and family, William Burgess and family, and John Davis and family expressed a desire to join the church. So I could not take the books away, but turned them over to Fate Pryer. I then organized the Sunday school and called it Mount Olive.

MIDWAY

One day while I was teaching at Vredenburgh, a Baptist preacher, Cornelius Smith, came and informed me that he knew of a good place for a mission and that the people would be glad to have one of our missions there. I asked where the place was, and he told me it was across the Alabama River at Midway, on Judge B. M. Miller's place. I asked for the names of some persons to whom I might write. He said I might write to C. P. Smith, Catherine, Alabama. I was informed that the chances for building a Lutheran church in Midway were just as good as at any place in Alabama and that he would be glad to have us.

I sent this letter to Rev. Bakke and wrote across the back "Special Attention." He wrote in haste that I should go to Midway. I did not go at once, as I wished to see Judge Miller and have his consent before going there. Judge Miller was then the circuit judge. When he came to Camden for court that fall, I went to see him. He granted me the privilege to go to Midway at once.

I set a date to go, but on that date there was a death in the family of the people with whom I was boarding. Therefore I had no one to take me, and the only other way would have been to go by way of Selma, which would have cost a good bit of money. Unwilling to make big traveling expenses for the Mission Board, I canceled that appointment and decided to wait for a more convenient time.

I succeeded in getting a team and went to Cobb's Landing and then crossed the Alabama to Midway. That Sunday, the first in December, I addressed a large audience in St.

Michael's Baptist Church, representing my church and its great mission work. When my speech was ended, the people sang a plantation song, "O Lord, won't you come by here? O Lord, won't you come by here?" with the usual refrain.

From Midway I went directly to Rev. Bakke at Oak Hill and made my report. The old Gospel veteran arose and went to Midway, December 7, carrying with him the Sunday school books. The following March I received a letter at Vredenburgh from Pastor Bakke, telling me to pack my things and go to Midway. I arrived in Midway March 18, 1917, opened the day school, and called it Mount Carmel. How strange that the request for the establishment of this church came from a Baptist minister who never became a member of the Lutheran Church!

TILDEN, DALLAS COUNTY

One day during the summer of 1916 Brother Ollie Ramsey met my brother Sam Young on the street in Selma and told him about our Lutheran church at Rosebud. Brother Sam became interested, saddled his horse, and came over to see me. I encouraged him, and he went to Rev. Bakke. He was commissioned to return to Tilden to see what could be done. Amid adverse circumstances and persecution, Brother Sam influenced a number of people to give their names to receive Christian instruction and join the church. Rev. Bakke went to Tilden on November 12, 1916, and organized a Lutheran church and Sunday school, which he called Mount Calvary, under a large, beautiful water oak which stood in Brother Sam's yard. Thereafter the tree was called the Holy Oak.

INGOMAR

One day Director Drewes was visiting our mission at Tilden. After services he walked about the grounds, talking to Brother

Sam, at that time the teacher there. He raised his hand and, pointing toward Ingomar, said, "Sam, are there people living away over in that direction?"

"Hundreds of them," answered Sam.

"Well, can't you go over there and start another mission for us?" said Director Drewes.

After that day, Brother Sam went to Ingomar, rented a house, and got a large crowd together. They borrowed some lumber from a sawmill near by, carried it over to the house on their backs, and there arranged it for seats. Then they sent for Rev. Bakke. He answered their call at once. May 11, 1919, he preached the first pure Gospel sermon in Ingomar and organized a Lutheran mission, which he called Grace. After the service, Sam and the people shouldered the borrowed lumber and carried it back to the sawmill.

Grace, Ingomar, has disappeared, but I am constrained to write of it as a mark of God's wrath upon those who rejected the pure Gospel. Yet God's Word did not return unto Him void. Some faithful members who established their residence elsewhere are members of our Lutheran congregations in the North, the East, and the South.

NYLAND

One day while I was teaching school at Midway, I looked out of the schoolroom window and noticed a crowd of people coming toward the school. There were so many people I hardly knew what to think. I just stood stock-still. When the crowd arrived, I found to my surprise that it was a delegation from Nyland, asking that a mission be begun at Nyland, nine miles from Midway. I dismissed my classes and held an instruction meeting with them. Shortly after they had left the school, a great tempest arose and scattered the band. That night they had to seek refuge wherever they could, reaching home the next morning after wading through mud and water.

I arranged to go to Nyland and have a meeting with the people. That Friday night I had the opportunity to speak to a large audience, representing my Church and its work. They voted for a mission. I reported this to Rev. George A. Schmidt. He went to Nyland on February 8, 1918, and organized a Lutheran mission and called it Bethany.

TAIT'S PLACE

While I was teaching at Midway, a delegation of two men, Walter Hill and Willie Kennedy, came to my Sunday school one Sunday morning, seeking a Lutheran mission. I had instructions with them and made a date to go over and speak to their people. I had the privilege of representing my Church before a large crowd there. They also voted for a mission. I sent this report to Rev. Schmidt. He went to Tait's Place and organized Zion mission the night of October 7, 1919. The first meeting place was a dilapidated log church which was owned by the colored Methodists.

St. John's, Joffre, was organized after a young teacher, Mrs. Pearl Deramus, had visited a service at Rosebud and was so impressed by what she heard that she did not rest until the Lutheran Church came to her community.

Gethsemane, Hamburg, was organized at the invitation of the white people of the community. Two confirmed members who had moved from Oak Hill and Tilden were the first members.

Pilgrim, Birmingham, is the only fully self-supporting congregation in the Alabama Field. It was started by the C. P. Smith family that had formerly been members at Mt. Carmel, Midway, and had moved to Birmingham. This congregation had 207 baptized members and 137 communicants in 1946.

Faith, Mobile, is also a result of mission work done by members of Mt. Carmel, Mrs. Viola Williams and her daughter Elizabeth. The first pastor was the Rev. R. O. L. Lynn. The congregation numbered 320 baptized members and 146 communicants in 1946. There were 130 in the Sunday school and 102 in the two-teacher Christian day school.

Concordia, Montrose, was started with a small group of Lutherans who had moved from Tinela.

Holy Cross, Camden, was organized by Superintendent E. A. Westcott for the sake of several Lutherans who had moved into Camden from Our Savior Congregation at Possum Bend.

Jehovah, Pensacola, Fla., was begun through the efforts of Emma Martin of Rosebud, who had been confirmed by the sainted Pastor Nils J. Bakke. The congregation is a very active one and gives every promise of becoming self-supporting.

Ebenezer, Atmore, is a result of mission work done by the two brothers of the McCant sisters who had caused the church to be organized at Vredenburgh.

Trinity, Selma, was established soon after the Alabama Lutheran Academy was located there. In 1946 there were nearly 200 in the Sunday school and more than 100 in the Christian day school.

St. Timothy, East Selma, was established entirely for the unchurched of this very needy section of Selma.

St. Philip's, Catherine, is another child of Mt. Carmel, Midway, having been established at the earnest request of the late James and Sally Scott, who had been confirmed at Midway.

Hope, King's Landing, owes its beginning to an ex-slave, Aunt Rosa. Aunt Rosa heard her first Lutheran sermon in Selma. Though a cripple, she went about her neighborhood telling men and women about the Lutheran Church, and with such enthusiasm and interest that Hope Church was organized to serve her community.

Bethel, Rockwest, is a branch of Zion, Tait's Place, which is not far away.

Bethlehem, Holy Ark, being only eight miles from Joffre, was organized after the Durden and Smith families had visit- ed the services at Joffre, and become interested in the Luth- eran Church.

Our Redeemer, Longmile, was a result of mission work done by the mother of Rev. P. R. Hunt, an active pastor on the Alabama field.

St. Mark's, Ackerville, was purely a mission project, started by one of our parochial school teachers, Mrs. Augusta Griffin.

St. Luke, Lamison, was organized as a result of mission work done by an ex-slave, Aunt Fanny Steele, who had learned to know her Savior when she took instruction and was confirmed at Nyland.

St. Peter's, Pine Hill, was organized to reach the people of that village who had become interested in the church by visit- ing Nyland.

St. Matthew, Arlington, is another result of the personal mission efforts of Aunt Fanny Steele of Nyland and Lamison.

Peace, Maplesville, in its conception reminds one of the Bible story of Philip and the Eunuch. Pastor R. O. L. Lynn was driving from Birmingham to Selma when he offered a ride to an old man on the highway. The pastor used the op- portunity to tell the man about Jesus. The old man told the people of his community about the ride and the visit with the Lutheran pastor, and he kept repeating his story until finally a church was built in order that all the people might have a chance to hear the Gospel. A choice plot of land was given the Missionary Board by Dr. H. M. Nix for a new chapel.

Messiah, Bashi, was organized at the request of Mrs. Davis, mother of Mattie Davis and Mrs. Geraldine Adams, two of our successful Lutheran teachers.

Good Shepherd, Vineland, was another mission project begun by Rev. P. R. Hunt while he was pastor at Bashi.

Calvary, Maysville, is a recently organized church, the result of mission work done by Pastor Wm. G. Kennell and his assistants.

Expansion. Mission work has also been started at Freemanville, Beloit, Thomasville, Sweet Water, Snow Hill, and Greenville, Ala., at Pascagoula, Miss., and at Oakfield, Fla.

One can see at a glance how the Lord sent delegations to us, one after the other, which sought our Lutheran Zion. Therefore the following Bible verse can well be applied to the Black Belt: "Arise, therefore, and get thee down, and go with them, doubting nothing; for I have sent them."

14

SOME OF MY EXPERIENCES
AS A PIONEER WORKER

•

Be strong and of a good courage; be not afraid, neither be thou
dismayed; for the Lord, thy God, is with thee
withersoever thou goest
JOSH. 1:9

•

THE VERY DAY ON WHICH I SEVERED MY RELATIONS WITH THE
African Methodist Church and joined the Evangelical Lutheran Church, willing to work for Jesus, was the day on which
the devil turned the people against me. The host of friends I
had in the sectarian churches deserted me. The good reputation I had was attacked by the enemy. I was left, so to speak,
alone, a friendless creature in this wide, wide world. Among
the hundreds of letters which I receive annually there are even
to this day hardly any from those colored people with whom
I formerly was affiliated.

The leaders in the sectarian churches pledged themselves to
overthrow the Lutheran Church. One preacher announced
that he would be a wasp in my garments as long as I lived;
but the poor man is dead now. They held meetings and coun-
cils one after another against me. They never held a service or
an annual meeting but that there was something mean said
about me. They hung out my name at evil's door. Preachers
stood up and proclaimed from their pulpits, "Rosa Young is a
devil." Others proclaimed, "Rosa Young hath a devil." "Rosa
Young is a Jezebel, an antichrist, a false prophet." "Rosa
Young is a Democrat; she is working for the white people.

She is an old white-man woman; she is not fit to lead you-all. She is not fit to teach your children." All this slander sank into my heart like so many arrows.

From polished preachers and professors down to rude stable boys, people heaped slander upon me and my work. Whenever I succeeded in getting up a class for confirmation or Baptism, the enemies would unite their powers to break it up. They would go around and stir up the people by telling them that the Lutheran Church was going to put them all back under slavery if they sent their children to our schools. They said that after a certain length of time the Lutherans were going to send a black train through and take all the children away into some far country and reduce them to slavery. These reports would cause great excitement. The enemies would go about and say that the Lutheran Church would cut off the children's ears, brand an L on them with a red-hot iron as a mark of their denomination. Numbers of the poor, ignorant people believed this. The dreamers went out and reported that they had been to hell and had seen Rosa Young there yoked down with all the people who had followed her into the Lutheran Church; that Rosa Young was tearing up the churches; that she was leading the people to hell for money; that she ought to be Klu-kluxed, skinned alive, burned at the stake. What could I say or do to all this but remain silent? It went on until it finally shocked my nerves.

The people turned against me. I could not get a kind word or favor from my old friends. One afternoon I was obliged to go to Camden to buy some things for one of our missions. I could not get a train out until the next morning; so I had to stay overnight. Sad to say, not one family in Camden among my former friends would let me remain in their home overnight. I wandered about on the streets that night until nearly eleven o'clock, trying to find a place to stay overnight. At last a little woman, a newcomer in Camden, whose husband was a sawmill man, sitting out on the porch waiting for her husband to come home from his work, spoke to me and said, "You can stay with me, lady."

I was so glad that I could have shouted for joy. I went into the house. She had but one bed, in which she and her husband slept. She offered me this, but I did not wish to rob them of their bed; so I declined and accepted a pallet on the floor.

When I went into these different communities to work up a mission, I was always obliged to find shelter or lodging with the most humble people, because the enemy had gone into the various sections before me and poisoned the minds of the better class or regular churchgoing people. So the people who were really able to care for a teacher looked upon our Church with contempt and scorn.

In many of the crude homes in which I had to board, I suffered great discomforts. Many a time I did not have sufficient bedding to keep myself warm and comfortable on cold nights. I had to retire with all my clothes on, except shoes and hat. Many a morning I had to leave for school and teach all day without a morsel to eat, for the host had nothing in the house with which to prepare a meal. On some days I would have two meals, on others one, and on still others none. At times I would become so hungry that I would go out into the pastures and eat blackberries, plums, and dewberries. During the winter months I would have nowhere to go to seek food, for the fields were dry and dead. Sometimes I would look at the roofs of all the houses in the community and wonder in which one I could get a piece of bread to eat if I should go there and ask for it.

Why did I not send to the store? Sometimes I was too far away from the stores and had no way of reaching them save on foot. At other times I did not have a penny with which to buy food. As my salary at that time was only $20 a month, nothing would be left save my railway fare home after I had paid my board, purchased a few clothes and the necessary books, and laid aside my contributions for the church.

During those dark days of suffering for bodily needs I had to go visiting in order to reach the people. Visiting is the key to success in mission work. It unlocks the door of opportunity where you may enter many a home and tell the people the old, old story of Jesus and His love. I had no conveyance to carry me from place to place except my feet. Sometimes I would walk all day in the cold wind or in the hot sun or through rain, mud, water, and sandbeds, through dense forests and swamps, over hills, across creeks and streams, to reach my people and deliver a Gospel message.

In some communities in which I worked I could once in a while rent a horse to ride. Sometimes I would start out from home on horseback and ride all day, going from house to house, and when I dismounted at night, I would be so sore and stiff that I could not stand up when my feet touched the ground. I would just fall to the ground.

Once I was asked by Rev. Bakke to go to a new place to begin work. I had to go by railway and change trains at a certain junction. When I reached the junction, I learned that the train was late. It was due to arrive at the junction at eight o'clock, but did not get there until midnight. There was no railway station there, only a small place where the conductor would go for a few moments to attend to his railroad affairs. I was the only lady to leave the train; one man alighted also, and there were several colored men waiting for the arrival of the next train. It was due from Centry, Florida, and they were expecting some whisky. All the men went into the little room, but I remained standing outside. I stood there so long that white frost formed all over the top of my hat, and I was nearly chilled through.

I reached my destination the next morning about eight o'clock, as I had to change trains once more.

Once I was boarding with a young couple, members of ours. They quarreled one night and parted, and the husband left the home. The next day I went down to the church and stayed there until night, when the sexton came to repair the church bell. I told him of my trouble, and he took me to his home. His wife bade me welcome at her home and baked some corn bread, while her husband went to the store and bought a box of sardines. That night I had bread and sardines for supper. I used the sexton's pocket knife, as there was no tableware in the house. Such poverty is found in many, many homes down here.

When I was ready to retire, the lady took me into another room, where there was a large pile of seed cotton they had picked that fall. In a corner there was piled an old bed which they had taken down to destroy the bedbugs. My host leveled the pile smoothly and spread a quilt over it. He turned over a large cotton-picking basket, and I seated myself upon that for a chair. I sank so deep into the cotton, and I was so tired, that I felt as though I were sitting in a reed rocker.

At one place where I boarded, the room was so open that I had to put on my raincoat and stretch my umbrella over myself at night in bed to keep from getting wet when it rained. Once I boarded with a non-Lutheran family, and because I would not partake of the Lord's Supper in their church, my host put me out. About sunset that evening I walked to another home and told the lady that the foxes have holes, the birds of the air have nests, but that I had no place to lay my head. She invited me in. I remained there three months; but because I would not attend her church, I had to move again.

At one place we had only a few female members, and all were somewhat dull; there was not much get-up about them. One of those women died. Not one of our members could shroud a person. I went to the non-Lutherans, but they refused; so I had to go back and shroud the woman myself. It was the first time I had ever touched a dead person. At the grave I had to go among the crowd of men and beg some to help cover the grave.

Once I was at a place where I had to live in a church. I could find no home in the community. Two little motherless girls lived with me. During the day the little girls would go home to help work in the fields and return at night. We cooked our meals on the heater. One evening Pastor Drewes came there to visit me. We were cooking on our heater when we heard that he was coming. We were ashamed to have him find us cooking there; so we hurried out of the room with our skillet of meat and hid it under the church. We hurried so fast to have the skillet hidden before Director Drewes reached the place that after he was gone, we couldn't find it at first; and the bad part of it was that when we did find it, a dog had eaten all our meat. All three of us stood there stock-still, for we had no more meat. That night we had bread and water for supper.

I was afraid to raise the windows at night; so during the hot weather I suffered much for lack of fresh air. One night, about midnight, some passers-by came along. The little girls were fast asleep, but I was still awake, as I did not sleep much in that church. The passers-by began to whistle to each other as they approached the church. They drew nearer and reached the door. They made a curious noise at the door. I remained silent. Then I heard them say, "They are not here." My heart beat fast as I prayed to the Lord to protect us.

One night I was at the church cooking my and the little girls' supper. I was alone, as they had gone to sell black-berries. Suddenly I grew afraid. I went out to ring the church bell (the brethren had told me to do so if anything disturbed me); but I was not able to do so as the wind had blown the rope onto the top of the church. I returned indoors and continued with the cooking for a while. Finally I be-came so frightened that I ran from the church to the home of the nearest neighbor until the little girls came.

At another time I was at a place where my Church was accused of being a German Church. It was during the World War. There was great excitement, and a number of the mem-bers in fear denied, like Peter, that they belonged to the Lutheran Church or knew anything about it. When the news reached me, I gathered together all my religious books and carried them to those in authority. I took along the letter I had received from Booker T. Washington in order to prove to them that the Lutheran missionaries were no spies or intruders and that I was the whole cause and was to blame for it that they were in Alabama. The first day I did not suc-ceed in getting a hearing, but I returned the second day and was successful. I presented Booker T. Washington's letter to them. They kept it, and thus I lost possession of that im-portant letter.

After that the Hon. J. T. Dale of Oak Hill wrote to them and settled the excitement. The Hon. J. T. Dale, Mr. J. Lee

Bonner, Judge B. M. Miller, and Mr. Dennis Forte were instruments in the hands of God to save our Mission in wartimes. They helped us win an important battle.

15

WHAT THE LUTHERAN CHURCH HAS
DONE FOR THE COLORED PEOPLE

•

*So shall My Word be that goeth forth out of My mouth; it shall
not return unto Me void, but it shall accomplish that which
I please, and it shall prosper in the thing whereto I sent it*
Is. 55:11

•

GOD'S WORD IS ALWAYS THE SAME. THESE WORDS SPOKEN
through Isaiah to the world hundreds of years ago are
just as true today as they were then, as is clearly manifested
in our mission work on the Alabama field in these last evil
days.

You have read in the previous chapters how our Lutheran
Church came to Alabama, an unknown Church, in the midst
of wartimes and in the face of great persecution and slander.
The Lord's Word proclaimed by the missionaries did not return to Him void, but went forth and accomplished that
which He pleased and prospered in the thing whereto He sent
it. We had in the Alabama Field, in 1946, thirty-five colored
Lutheran congregations and several preaching places. Of
these, two churches were in Florida and one in Mississippi; all
the rest in Alabama. At these thirty-five places, where the
Bread of Life was being broken to old and young, we had a
total membership of 3,212 souls, all live, active members of
the Savior's Church in the Black Belt. Just think of it, a few
years ago this vast number of people had never heard of the
Lutheran Church.

The above figures do not represent all the people our Church is reaching through our day schools, divine services, Sunday schools, midweek instruction meetings, literature, and missionary visits. In every community where our Lutheran Church is established the seed of God's Word is sown upon the hearts of hundreds of persons not listed in our mission records. Through the religious books, especially the Catechism and the Bible History, which the children carry into their homes, many mothers, fathers, relatives, and friends learn to know of Jesus and His great love for sinners. Once a young woman came to our superintendent and asked to be taken into the Lutheran Church. He asked where she had learned about the Lutheran Church and why she wished to join it. She answered that her little brothers were attending the Lutheran school in East Selma, and through them she had learned to know and love the Lutheran Church.

God alone knows how much glorious Gospel light has illumined hundreds of formerly dark and dreary cabins through the religious schoolbooks the children carry into their homes. Old and young into whose ears and hearts the Word of God has sounded rejoice in the knowledge, yes, the saving knowledge, of a loving Savior who died on the Cross for their sins.

In the thirty schools of the Black Belt there were in 1946, 26 female teachers, 3 male teachers, and 5 pastors, teaching 1,227 children the Word of God. Our Sunday schools in the same year had an enrollment of 1,657 pupils who were learning the Word of God. Streams of blessings flow from these nurseries into the cabins of ignorance and sin of the colored people here in the Southland.

The Lutheran Church with its pure Gospel is stirring every community in which it has been established. Both Lutherans and non-Lutherans have felt the effects of it. The power and influence of the unadulterated Word of God which she is proclaiming has transformed people into wholly new and different creatures. The people who have come in contact with our Lutheran Church and have not hardened their hearts against its divine teaching are radically different. They speak, act, think, and look different. They see things in a different light. It is marvelous, showing the great power of God's Word. They are the same people, possessing the same bodies, reason, judgment, and senses as before, but they are transformed beings in every way and seem to be living in a new world.

The colored people in their natural state are a noisy people; they love noise; they praise noise; they applaud and approve noise. If one wishes to succeed with the colored people, he must be noisy. The more noise he makes, the more quickly he will succeed. One has to be a real novelist, keeping something new before them all the time. As a rule the colored people will join any group that presents itself. And they have a tendency to break away from any person or any group that tries to make them pious.

Those who know the colored people in their unconverted state can hardly imagine them in a church that holds a quiet, decent, orderly service. But the Lutheran Church has changed them, and now they rejoice that the Word of God has been sown in their hearts. The teaching in the Sunday schools and in the day schools has changed them completely. God's Word has not returned to Him void. It really has accomplished that which He pleased and has prospered in the thing whereunto He sent it. Those who have hearkened to God's Word, who have not hardened their hearts, have truly been transformed from the children of Satan into the children of God.

They think and speak differently and look like new persons. They live in a new world.

The Lutheran Christian hymns of praise to Jesus are fast taking the place of the old plantation melodies in the homes, schools, churches, and in the fields. Since the Lutheran Church has come into the Black Belt with the pure Gospel of Jesus Christ, a number of colored people who previously never thought of God's Word are reading the Bible daily. In homes where parents and children once lived in hellish riot, in homes where hatred, anger, vice, shame, sin, adultery, fornication, and theft prevailed, there has been a great change through the power of God, and they have become Christian homes. In many a home in which formerly no Christian hymn had ever been sung, no prayer uttered, and no Bible read, there is now a family altar morning and evening. Also the colored Lutherans attend the Lord's Supper gladly.

The Lutheran Church has even thrown light on the sectarian churches around it. They do not conduct those noisy revivals as they did before the Lutheran Church came into the Black Belt. Those revivals were actually horrible. The people were told that in order to find Christ, they must go into the woods, fields, and graveyards; that they must quit eating, drinking, bathing, and changing their garments; that they must quit speaking to people, tie up their heads, cover their faces, pull off their shoes, and go mourning all their days to find Jesus and peace for their souls; that when they were converted, they would know this of themselves, for they would hear strange noises and see strange sights; they would then go to hell and see the devil and his angels; they would walk across hell on a spiderweb; the hellhounds would run them all the way back from hell to earth again; they would go to heaven and see Jesus and talk with Him of their troubles.

Now, if a convert failed to see, hear, and do any of these strange things, he was considered unconverted and was refused membership in the church.

Another way the sectarian churches had of securing Christians was to manufacture them. A long bench called the mourners' bench was placed in front of the pulpit. All of those who were seeking religion would be obliged to go up and take their seats on that bench. After the preacher had ended his sermon, the mourners would kneel down, and all the members and the preacher would gather about them, stamping their feet, clapping their hands, holloing and praying at the top of their voices. Sometimes all the members in the church would be praying at the same time, just as loud as they could. Many a time the mourners were nearly frightened out of their wits.

Since the Lutheran Church has come into the Black Belt with the pure Gospel and lighted these dark sections, the big revivals are fast losing ground. The people's eyes have been opened to the true way of salvation. The people who walked in darkness have seen a great light. Even the sectarian preachers themselves no longer force this way of conversion as strongly as before. One sectarian preacher who had preached to the people for some thirty years stood up and said publicly: "Oh, if I had the opportunity to go back over all those sermons which I have preached, I would pick out all the false doctrine and tell you the truth." Another preacher confessed: "We know that we have not been preaching the Bible, the truth, to you people. We just preached to suit you all; but from now on I, for my part, am going to preach the Bible."

Thank God also for the blessings that have come to sectarian churches through Lutheran preaching!

16

SOME ZEALOUS, FAITHFUL MEMBERS

•

"Be ye doers of the Word and not hearers only." "I will
show you my faith by my works"
James 1:22; 2:18

•

PERMIT ME TO POINT OUT A FEW EXAMPLES OF PERSONS WHO
had been on the wrong road to heaven, but who became
honored members of the Lutheran Church. There was

OLD "UNCLE" SIMON

He learned the true way to heaven in the evening of his
life; for "Uncle" Simon was an old, gray-haired man, wrinkled
and stooped with the burden of some eighty-odd years when
he learned the true way to heaven.

"Uncle" Simon was not a vile sinner; he was a member of
another church, a deacon for forty years. He was honored
and loved by both white and colored alike. A white man who
owns one of the largest plantations in Wilcox County told our
superintendent that he knew of no other person in whom he
had greater confidence than "Uncle" Simon. He had a peaceful home, where both men and women went for advice and
where little children went to play. He tried hard to keep
God's holy Law; but there was one thing lacking—"Uncle"
Simon did not know his Savior. It was on February 19, 1922,
in Sid McDowell's home on the Longmile place, where Rev.
Schmidt preached the first Lutheran sermon, that "Uncle"
Simon's blinded eyes were opened to the true way of salvation.
He testified to that fact himself when he said: "If the Luther-

an Church had not come, I would have gone to hell." "Uncle" Simon fell asleep in Jesus on August 19, 1924.

BETTIE SKINNER

Bettie Skinner testifies that she was troubled about her sins and her inability to keep God's holy Law. Like the dove let out of the ark that could find no rest for the sole of its feet, so Bettie Skinner could find no rest or peace for her heart and conscience. Yes, she had tried other churches in a vain effort to find something that would quiet that annoying and accusing voice within. Neither the church to which she belonged nor any other could give her soul the desired relief. Her husband, who was a preacher in the church to which she belonged, could not help her. In her earnest but vain endeavors she asked others to give her a truly satisfying answer to the question "What must I do to be saved?" She was tossed about with fears and doubts and misgivings, for the load of sin she carried was oppressive, and the future looked dark for her.

It was in 1923 that God led Bettie Skinner to a Lutheran church one night, when a meeting was being held in an old rented house in Selma. The Lutheran pastor spoke of the forgiveness of sins and directed those present to the Lamb of God, slain for sinners, with whose blood God wipes out all their sins. While the pastor was proclaiming the pure Word, the Holy Ghost entered Bettie Skinner's heart and opened her eyes to the sufficiency of Christ's blood and God's mercy. After the meeting she said: "I never knew that wonderful truth before. Everything looks so different now." She joined the Lutheran Church.

Later she was given a position in one of our schools. Fired with love for the Savior and anxious to bring to others the gladsome message of the Savior's kingdom, she labored faithfully in the cause for many years.

"Aunt" Fannie

Like thousands of other colored people, "Aunt" Fannie Steele lived in a little hut among the pine-covered hills near Nyland. Her eyes were growing dim, her body weak, her limbs feeble. Sitting in her homemade rocker by the fireplace during the long, rainy winter days and evenings, she had time to think, yes, to think as she had never thought before. Looking back, it was clear the world had not given her pleasure and wealth. A glance about the room in which she sat was convincing. Then there were her sins; many, many of them she could still recall. They troubled her. What should she do? Beckoning her not far away was the grave—and the Judgment. Not a pleasant thought for "Aunt" Fannie. She was afraid to die.

The news of the meetings held on Tuesday nights at Nyland in a log cabin by a Lutheran preacher reached the ears of this old grandma one night as she sat in her rocker by the fireplace. It stirred her into action. She came to hear. She came again and again. Glorious words she heard, words about a Savior, a gracious, loving Savior, who died for sinners. God's Spirit sealed the message in her heart and made her happy. Now she could cherish a hope, the glorious hope of everlasting life in heaven. Gazing into the flames playing about the burning logs in the fireplace, she thought such happy thoughts of Jesus, her Savior; thoughts of forgiveness through His blood and salvation through Him; thoughts of the home eternal in the heavens.

Poverty drove "Aunt" Fannie for shelter to the home of a daughter miles away from her Lutheran church, but she refused to be separated from it. She could not read the Bible. The more reason why she should hear her pastor preach. What mattered it that she must use her few pennies for a railroad ticket; that early in the morning, when it was still dark, she must stumble along the road to find the station; that, because she had no clock, she would arrive at the railroad station hours before traintime?

"Aunt" Fannie attended the Lutheran services. God strengthened her and increased her faith. She became a shining light in the sin and darkness of the Black Belt. Her heart was full of Christ; it overflowed with gratitude to God; she incessantly talked about her Lutheran Church on the road, in the homes, wherever she happened to be. Her faith also bore fruit; for it was through her that our Lutheran Church came to Lamison and to Arlington.

PATSEY BENSON

"Aunt" Patsey Benson had never joined a church. She was born in the time of slavery. During the Civil War her husband disappeared, never to return. What happened to him no one knows. "Aunt" Patsey spent her days alone in a little one-room hut.

Before her conversion "Aunt" Patsey was a mean, selfish, and even a dangerous person. She cursed and would get furious over the slightest provocation. For this reason, people had nothing to do with her; so she lived near the woods. Nothing seemed to make her more angry than if some one would tell her about God and heavenly things. It is reported that she even threw hot water and irons at those who attempted to speak to her about her soul.

The first time the Lutheran preacher, Rev. John Thompson, approached her, he greeted her. In answer to his greeting, "Aunt" Patsey replied, "Who is you? I ain't got no time to be worried with you all!"

The pastor answered, "We'll wait until you have finished your work."

"Aunt" Patsey left the room, saying, "Don't you let me find you here when I come back!"

The missionary obeyed orders and left. Others watched and laughed. A few days later Rev. Thompson returned. "Aunt" Patsey saw him coming and closed her door. Several times the missionary called at her little hut, but no answer came from behind the closed door. Several more times the missionary called.

One cold morning Rev. Thompson arose with "Aunt" Patsey on his mind. He went to her home. The door was closed, but as it was so early, the missionary was convinced that she could not be far away. He looked about and spied her at the foot of a steep hill with a load of wood in her arms. When "Aunt" Patsey saw the missionary, she stood still, but said nothing. He went down the hill and carried the wood to the cabin, chopped it, and carried it into the cabin. Then it was that the first kind words fell from the lips of "Aunt" Patsey. "Well," said she, "you are good for something after all."

The missionary took this opportunity to tell her of the One who had done far more for her than he. "Aunt" Patsey replied, "Well, you will have to come another time to tell me about that."

A few days later the missionary returned and told "Aunt" Patsey that he had a letter to read to her. He began reading from the Gospel according to St. John. To show that she was not listening to him, "Aunt" Patsey went about her house singing and humming her peculiar melodies. This she continued to do during several visits which the missionary made after this.

One evening, to the missionary's surprise, "Aunt" Patsey seemed to have been waiting for him. She gave him a box to sit upon and sat down beside him, ready to listen to a lesson from the Bible. The missionary sent a prayer to the Throne of Grace. He spoke seriously to her about her soul, about sin, hell, damnation, forgiveness, salvation, and heaven. God blessed those words as He had on the previous occasion. "Aunt" Patsey was crushed and asked to be received into the church. On December 13, 1927, she was admitted as a member. Think of it, being baptized when over ninety years of age!

SALLIE SCOTT

Mrs. Scott was a faithful, God-fearing Lutheran from the day of her confirmation until the day of her death. Through her and her husband, James Scott, our church was organized at Catherine. Mrs. Scott was not well to do. She made a living by serving in the homes of white people. She was born a slave. After she obtained her freedom, she finally saved enough money to buy a few acres of land. She had always wanted to do something for the Lord. Therefore she made a will in which she gave to St. Philip's Congregation at Catherine four acres of land. She gave what she had.

James, the husband of Sallie Scott, was not a Christian when they were married, but his wife won him for Christ and the Lutheran Church. He was chairman of the Board of Deacons for many years, and died in that office.

MARIAH DOCKERY

Mariah was born in slavery, but her master's children had taught her to read and write. At a very great age she became a member of our Lutheran Church at Possum Bend. She never grew weary of telling others what she had learned about Jesus. If a Sunday school teacher was absent, she was always ready to volunteer her service as a teacher, though her ability was necessarily limited. She was so filled with the Holy Ghost that when her pastor or the field superintendent came to comfort her in her last illness, she would rather comfort them. Her last words were: "Lord, have You come? Come on, Lord; I have been waiting for You." Thus, Mother "Dock," as she was affectionately called, fell asleep in Jesus.

MILLER YOUNG

Miller, youngest brother of the author, was the first man to give Pastor Bakke his name for church membership in the State of Alabama. However, his work took him away from Rosebud, and he was not confirmed until twenty years later, when the congregation was organized at Hamburg. In all these twenty years he was trying to find a way to be saved, but no one had shown him. This he learned in the Lutheran Church, and thus he was able to die in Christ.

FLOWERS FOR THE LIVING

Madeira Ramsey, youngest sister of the author, is one of God's children in the Rosebud congregation. She has learned by the Holy Spirit to put first things first. The cause of Christ and her work in the church have first place in her life. No day is too cold, no night too dark, no wind too rough, for her to answer the call to help someone in the name of Christ. She is also a charter member of the mother church.

THE CARSTARPHEN FAMILY

Johnny Carstarphen and his family are leaders in our St. Paul's Congregation at Oak Hill. These Christian parents have had their six children baptized in the church; two have been married there; and it is the wish of these devoted followers of Christ that all the six be married and buried in the same church in which they were baptized. Two daughters are college graduates, two are in college, and two are yet in the Christian day school. One daughter is the wife of a Lutheran pastor. This family has been blessed with more of material things than most of our colored families, but they are generous supporters of the church and charitable toward their fellow men. Their hospitable home is always open to pastors, superintendents, and friends. We pray for more such faithful Lutheran Christians.

RUBY MAE CLEASENT

We joyfully present this young lady, a niece of the author, who was born, reared, and educated in the Lutheran Church. From her earliest childhood days she was interested in mission work. She taught in our Christian day schools three years. During a summer vacation she went to Detroit, where she met a young man from Abyssinia, Africa. She is now happily married to the man who was a trained minister in the Church of Christ. By the help of the Lord her husband has been won to the Lutheran Church and expects to enter one of our seminaries to become a Lutheran pastor. Who knows but that the Lord may call him back to his home country, Ethiopia, where Christianity first came to Africa, to preach the pure Lutheran Gospel.

MRS. R. O. L. LYNN

Mrs. Lynn is an educator, an author, a real benefactor of our race. As a mother she has no superior. She is a model housekeeper. She and her beloved husband have trained their three children to love the good and pure and to seek the noblest thing in life, that is, Jesus. Out of love for her Savior and her race she gave an entire year of service to Alabama Lutheran Academy without pay.

MRS. LOU D. JENKINS

As matron of Alabama Lutheran Academy, Mrs. Jenkins gave nearly twenty-five years of faithful service to the Church. In 1923, as a young woman, she was confirmed and became a member of Trinity Congregation in Selma and dedicated the rest of her life to Christ as a Christian day school teacher. She taught at Rosebud, Tinela, Kingslanding, and Mobile and then became the matron at Alabama Lutheran Academy, where her devotion to her Savior was an uplifting influence to hundreds of girls, to whom she was a "mother." She fell asleep suddenly on February 18, 1947, and was buried at Allenton, Ala., her birthplace. The funeral service was held at Trinity Church in Selma, with the pastor, Rev. A. Dominick, officiating with Rev. P. R. Hunt. Her son is the Rev. R. F. Jenkins, assistant pastor at Trinity and instructor in Alabama Lutheran Academy. Three daughters also survive. May the many who knew her be inspired through her example by the words of the Apostle: "For me to live is Christ and to die is gain," Phil. 1:21.

Now, dear readers, if the Lutheran Church in the Black Belt had brought no other fruit than the saving of the souls of the few persons whom I have named, yes, if it had brought no other fruit than the saving of the soul of just a one-hour-old infant, it would be more than compensated for all the energy and money spent and all the prayers offered on the entire Alabama field. Think of the worth of a soul in the sight of God!

Just think what would have become of the 3,211 souls listed on our mission records if God had not sent the Lutheran Church into this benighted land! "Uncle" Simon declared that he would have gone to hell if the Lutheran Church had not come. Hundreds and hundreds of others, old, middle-aged, young men and young women, and little children are testifying to the same thing: "If the Lutheran Church had not come, I would have gone to hell." I am another witness to the same fact; for if the Lutheran Church had not come,

I should have gone to hell. Dear readers, oh, listen! Can you
not hear that great number of voices of the colored people
coming out of the Alabama graves, saying: "If the Lutheran
Church had not come to me, I should have gone to hell"?
Hush, listen! It is a voice of gratitude, a voice of thanks to
the dear members of our Lutheran churches who have by their
prayers and gifts of hard-earned money made it possible to
send to such people the saving message of an uplifted and
saving Savior. Hush, listen! It is a voice of pleading, asking
the dear white Lutheran Christians not to grow weary; a
voice urging them to continue in the blessed work of bringing
to thousands of their fellow beings who are still groping in
darkness the glorious Gospel of a loving Savior before they
sink into a Christless and hopeless grave.

To God, and to Him alone, be all glory for His blessing!
May He, for Christ's sake, further bless the work of His
Church in these last evil days, so that many more who are
now traveling on the road to everlasting ruin may be rescued
before it is too late!

Isaiah saw our sad condition when he proclaimed that
darkness had covered the earth and gross darkness the people.
God permitted the same Prophet to see the remedy; and he
opened his mouth and prophesied, saying: "The people that
walked in darkness have seen a great light; they that dwell in
the land of the shadow of death, upon them hath the light
shined." Is. 9:2.

17

ILLNESS

•

Come ye yourselves apart into a desert place and rest a while
MARK 6:31

•

DURING THE SUMMER MONTHS, WHEN I WAS NOT TEACHING
school, I made it a rule to visit every home in the community and also in the adjacent communities, both Lutheran
and non-Lutheran. I made a list of the names of the people
who did not belong to, or attend, any church. Such people
I called my mission-material, and I endeavored by the help
of the Lord to get them into my Church. As it was summer-
time, I would find the people mostly in the fields. Many times
they worked miles away from their homes; but no matter
where they were or who they were, men, women, or children,
I would find them and deliver my Bible message to them.

The message which I delivered was taken from the Bible
and was selected in this wise: Every morning I rose early
and had my devotions, in which I prayed the Holy Spirit to
be with me that day and to enlighten me by His Word, so that
I would be able to teach it to others in all its truth and purity.
I also asked the Holy Spirit to cause the pure Gospel message
I would deliver to sink into the hearts of all to whom I
would that day tell it. I would then choose a short Bible
verse, fill my hands with copies of the *Lutheran Pioneer,* our
mission magazine at the time, and with a prayer in my heart
I would set out on my mission tour, seeking souls for Jesus all
along the way.

I hunted lost souls for Jesus somewhat as I hunted for money to build and maintain my first school. I endeavored to tell this Bible message to every person I saw that day. No matter how long it took me to work up to the point in our chat or conversation where I could deliver my Bible verse, I would deliver it. When I had told my message to one person, I would proceed to another. I walked in prayer all along the way from one person to another, asking the Lord to bless the message of His Word as I delivered it.

On one of these mission tours in August, 1918, I became very ill. I left home very early one morning, before eating any breakfast, and went on foot to Robin's Place, which was several miles away from the plantation where I was boarding. I reached Robin's Place about nine o'clock on a hot day in August. By that time the people were all at work in the fields. I went from field to field, and by noontime I had visited all the people on the place. Then I went back to the Cade Place before the people went out to work that evening.

Seeing a few families still at their homes, I decided to visit them before they left for the fields and then return to my boarding place and rest the remainder of the day. I first approached the home of an old couple, ex-slaves and non-Lutherans. I was tired, hot, sweaty, and thirsty. The man came out and invited me in. During the conversation, in which I was trying to work my way up to the point at which I could deliver my Bible message, the old host asked me if I liked melons. Being very fond of melons, I readily replied, "Yes, sir."

"Fix her a piece," he said to his wife.

The kind old lady went to the kitchen and soon returned with a very fine, delicious piece of muskmelon on a white plate, with a towel to spread in my lap and a knife with which to eat the melon. I had eaten but a few mouthfuls when I felt somewhat sick. Feeling myself growing worse, I soon gave the fine dish of melon to the hostess and bade them good-by without even telling them that I was sick. There were two reasons why I did not inform the kind old people of the spell of sickness that had come over me. I thought they might fear that the melon which they had given me had caused my illness and would therefore feel bad about it, or they might insist on my remaining with them until it had grown a little cooler. But as I grew steadily worse, I decided that it would be best for me to go to my boarding place before I would be unable to walk at all.

I hurried through a large green pasture, lying down many times here and there in the shade of the trees I passed on my way and finally resting on the green grass under the burning sun, as there were no longer any trees to protect me. About sunset I finally reached my destination. From the time of that hot day in August, 1918, until 1927 I never saw another really well day, no matter where I was. Regardless of what I was doing or how well I looked, I was suffering somehow. Now, it was not the eating of that melon that caused my illness. I dare say this illness had been working in me for a long time, and it just happened to come on at this particular time when I was exhausted from the heat, thirst, hunger, and a walk of many a mile that day on the plantation.

When I reached my boarding place, I was quite sick, yet I refrained from making it known to anyone for fear someone might wickedly accuse the kind old lady of dealing foully with me, which would hurt the feelings of those good old people in case it would reach their ears.

I went on thus for several weeks, growing worse all the time, until finally I was forced to make an outcry and a

physician had to be called. To my great surprise he said I
was suffering from heart trouble and prostrated nerves,
brought on by hard study, work, worry, insufficient nourish-
ment, insufficient recreation and sleep, and unkind treatment.
He advised me to give up teaching, step out of the busy
stream of life, and let the current roll by. But I was so deeply
involved in my glorious mission work for Jesus that I
thought the physician spoke like a foolish man.

Not willing to give up my post and lay down the work
which I was doing for the Lord and my race, I continued to
do my work and carried around with me a sick body. Many
a night I was too sick to sleep; all the night I wrestled with
pain, without, however, making it known to anyone in the
home where I was boarding. The next morning I would arise
bright and early for school and teach all day, making my
usual mission visits in the afternoon. I kept up my private
studies and all my correspondence, and besides this all the
cares and perplexities of life pertaining to my work worried me
and bore down upon me. Meanwhile I was going regularly
from one physician to another, occasionally being obliged to
call in first one, then another. From 1918 to 1922 I was
treated by sixteen different doctors. In the effort to recover
my health I had just about spent all I had.

One Sunday in 1922 I sat down after church at Rosebud
to answer some letters of my Northern friends and work out
my monthly report, when I was suddenly attacked by the
same old complaint and became its victim in the first degree.
I probably would have died; but God, in His goodness and
mercy, sent Mrs. J. Lee Bonner, my old white friend to the
parsonage where I was boarding, with medicine, which gave
me relief until a physician could be called. Faithful Mrs.

Bonner! She did what she could. Pastor Peay came also and ministered to me.

After this serious attack I was convinced of the truth of the physician's diagnosis and came to the conclusion that I should come out of the schoolroom and rest a while. Shortly afterward Teacher John Thompson, now Pastor Thompson, arrived from New Orleans to take charge of the school. I was asked to go to Selma, to Alabama Lutheran Academy, to serve as matron. I gladly accepted the call, as I was willing to do something more for the Lord and my race, and I thought this would help out the Mission Board by ·saving them the expense of employing a matron.

I began this new work when the school opened its doors the first time, in November, 1922, and held out until spring, 1923, when I had another breakdown. I remember asking my girls to call up Superintendent Schmidt and tell him to come and look after them, as I was just as sick as I could be. Rev. Schmidt, faithful pastor, soon arrived and, coming to my bedside, pictured Jesus, my Savior, to me. I do not remember when he left the room or how long he was gone, but when I saw him again, he and Pastor Westcott were sitting by the fire watching me. When I looked up and saw those two faithful white pastors whom the Lord Jesus had sent there, my heart was so full I could have burst into tears, just to see how God will take care of us in spite of our unworthiness.

The next day I was sent to the hospital, where I spent ten days. One morning after my return Rev. Schmidt informed me that I had to accept a vacation. I wept bitterly a long time. I thought it was so very unkind of Rev. Schmidt to take me from my work. Rev. Schmidt wept also, but he insisted that I accept the vacation. This was the first vacation I had had since I began teaching in 1909. The Mission Board had offered me one month's vacation every year with salary, but I had been so deeply engrossed in my mission work that I could not see how I needed, or could afford, a vacation. I had always said that I could rest all I wanted right on the job.

I left the dormitory for my home at Hamburg the next day. I had come home for a vacation, but I did not have one altogether; for soon after my return home I began the Lutheran Sunday school at my home, out of which grew the Gethsemane Lutheran Mission at Hamburg.

In the fall of 1923 I resumed my work as matron and held out fairly well until the spring of 1924, when I had another breakdown. Again I was obliged to give up my work and go home. During the summer of 1924 I offered my resignation as matron at Selma. ·

Shortly after I had resigned my position as matron at Alabama Lutheran Academy, Dr. Palmer of Furman announced that I must undergo a surgical operation. This was a shock to me and to all who heard it. I soon made up my mind, however, to have the operation performed as I hoped in that way to recover my health, so that I might resume my mission work. My mother took me to the Good Samaritan Hospital in Selma. The Lutheran pastors—blessed and faithful pastors they are—know how to take care of their members. They know how and with what to approach their people when they are drawing near to their last hours of life. They did not fail to visit me and comfort me with God's Word and humble prayer. Pastors Peay, Lynn, Lehman, Weeke, and Schmidt told me so many beautiful things about heaven, about Jesus, the Savior, while I was there waiting for the operation to be performed that they drew my mind completely out of this world. I longed for the day of the operation; for I thought that on that day I was going to die. I was going to heaven and see my Jesus. Rev. Schmidt was the last pastor to visit my room before the operation. He chose the text "I am with you alway" (Matt. 28:20). That was the evening before the operation. After he left me, the words of that Bible passage remained with me. All through the night, whenever I awoke, the first words that came to my mind were: "I am with you alway."

Wednesday morning I was strapped down on the operating table at eight o'clock. I felt no fear. I was so glad because I thought Jesus was going to take me to heaven with Him that morning. The last thing I remember before I fell asleep was Rev. Schmidt's text: "I am with you alway." I was on the operating table . ur and a half hours. Four doctors were there. They were all able men and experienced in their profession.

When I was brought out of the operating-room, I saw my mother and knew her. She told me that I said: "Mama, I am going to die and leave you."

"Well, you will go to heaven," she answered.

"Where is Jesus?" said I.

She replied, "He is with you."

I then repeated the following:

> Jesus, Thou art a sinner's Friend;
> As such I look to Thee;
> Now in the bowels of Thy love,
> O Lord, remember me.

The second person I remember recognizing was Rev. Schmidt. He asked me what the text was that he had given me the night before. I told him: "I am with you alway."

My operation was such a serious one that I considered it a miracle that it was successful. God preserved my life. Dr.

Palmer told me later that at times he could not find my pulse, and then the operating surgeon would have to wait until my heart could gain more strength, sometimes from fifteen to twenty minutes at a time.

The next severe attack which I suffered after the operation was during the summer of 1925. Dr. Palmer had to make forty visits in succession. At one time he had to put me to sleep and let me sleep for two weeks. After this long sleep he let me awaken. When I awoke, I seemed to have lost control of myself to a great extent. I felt afraid that I would become insane; but the doctor said my mind was all right; my heart was sending the blood along the arteries so slowly that the brain was starving. That summer it was announced that I was deceased. Rev. Schmidt, the other pastors, and a few teachers came to lay my remains away to rest, but they found me alive.

The next attack I suffered was during the summer of 1926. That summer is one long to be remembered by me, for the attack was worse than the one I had the previous summer. Dr. Palmer had to make about one hundred visits to my bedside. I was speechless for a while and then became partly like an insane person. Dr. Palmer fought the case like a hero. He said he left me many a night not expecting ever to see me alive again. But Jesus preserved my life. Our missionaries spared no pains in keeping Jesus before me. They ministered to me faithfully. In 1927 I found relief to a great extent. Though I was sick most of the time, God allowed me to see some well days.

It is indeed a great thing to be a Christian. If I had not known my Savior and trusted Him as I did, where would I be today? Jesus has done great things for me. The Word of God which I had learned in our dear Lutheran Church was all that I had to depend upon, and in His Word I found comforting passages to suit every stage and condition of my sickness. The Holy Spirit brought all things I needed to my remembrance.

While suffering bodily, I also suffered persecution from my enemies. There were preachers in the sectarian churches who stood in their pulpits and laughed me to scorn, proclaiming: "It is good for her. God is punishing her for bringing the Lutheran Church into Alabama." They even dared their members to visit me in my sickness. Besides the persecution of the enemy I had to struggle with the devil, who was trying to prove to me that Jesus did not love me any more, that it was useless to try to still hold on. But the grace of the Lord Jesus was sufficient. My constant prayer was: "Thy will be done." I hereby wish to thank the church at large for ministering to me by word and deed.

18

BRIGHTER DAYS

•

*Fear thou not; for I am with thee. Be not dismayed; for I am thy
God. I will strengthen thee; yea, I will help thee; yea, I will
uphold thee with the right hand of My righteousness*
Is. 41:10

•

The year 1931 brought the dawn of a new day for me. The
time had come for me to leave the desert place of sickness. The
rest period was about over. I was to resume my place as a
worker in God's vineyard and take up mission work again
among my people. My health improved gradually, but I still
had to contend with a weak heart and overtaxed nerves.

One day I received unsolicited a bottle of medicine from a
pastor in Milwaukee. The medicine, made in Germany, was
highly recommended for a weak heart. I took the treatment
and noticed a rapid improvement. I rested well at night and
was able to visit almost daily.

One day a letter came from the Rev. G. W. Wolter of Arlington, Nebr., extending an invitation from the ladies' aids
for me to conduct a lecture tour in Northern Nebraska. He
also wrote to Director Christopher F. Drewes, who consulted
the Missionary Board. The matter was then left for me to
decide. I went. June 30, 1931, was a memorable day for me,
for it was on that day that I started on my first trip North. I
left Selma, Ala., at 7:30 in the morning for Birmingham,
where I visited for several hours with Pastor and Mrs. W. T.
Eddleman. Since I was to go through St. Louis, Pastor Eddle-

man wired the Rev. A. Schulze to meet me. I was sorry I had to travel all night and thus be deprived of enjoying the beautiful scenes along the way. There was nothing to break the silence of the night except the rumbling of the old iron horse as he rushed along and an occasional whistle as we sped through the smaller towns. When the morning dawned, I was very conscious of the fact that I was already far away from my Alabama home. The blue and purple flowers blooming on the beautiful hills in Arkansas, and the fields of corn and waving grain in Missouri, made a picture very different from the cotton fields of my native state. I arrived late on the 3d of July at the great Union Station in St. Louis. Finally, I was actually in St. Louis, the center of Lutheranism, a beautiful city with a thousand sights for me to see. I did not know Pastor Schulze, and he did not know me, but finally we found each other, and I was taken to the parsonage, where I met dear Mrs. Schulze and Paul. Pastor Schulze had arranged for me to speak to his Bible class.

The next day it was my privilege to see some of the great city of St. Louis. I tried to miss nothing as we drove through the busy streets. I was charmed by the beauty of it all, terraced lawns, green grass, stately buildings, schools, beautiful churches, huge parks with shaded promenades and shooting fountains; the famous zoo, where animals and birds have been brought from the far corners of the earth for the pleasure and entertainment of the thousands of children and grownups who visit the zoo in Forest Park; the world-famous Lindbergh trophies in the Jefferson Memorial Building in Forest Park; the Art Museum, one of the finest in the country; Shaw's Garden, where strange plants and flowers from all parts of the world create a panorama of rare charm and beauty; the great Concordia Seminary, perhaps the most beautiful buildings of their kind in America. One almost regrets that such truly beautiful structures cannot stand forever. Not only do the ivy covered stone walls, and towers, and spacious classrooms make these buildings unequaled in beauty, but things taught within the classrooms render the seminary unequaled in a far grander way.

But I had to be on my way to Nebraska. Again Pastor Schulze helped me by sending ahead a message that I would arrive in Omaha at a certain hour, so that my host, the Rev. G. W. Wolter, might be there to meet me. I had scarcely passed through the gates when I saw a man with a friendly smile approaching me. I was sure he was the man. Mrs. Wolter had come along, and after hearty greetings had been exchanged, we were on our way to Arlington.

Pastor Wolter, the man with a kind voice and a cheering smile, holds a warm spot in his heart for mission work among the colored. He acted as my director while I was lecturing in Nebraska. I was most welcome in their home, where Mrs. Wolter with a big Christian heart made everyone feel welcome in her presence. The four sons and daughters also were very kind and hospitable to me, and today I often refer to this quiet, peaceful parsonage as my Nebraska home.

The pastor had arranged for me to speak at certain churches where those from other near-by churches were invited to come. I lectured on Sunday afternoons, usually, and was thus enabled to spend most of the weekdays in quiet at the parsonage in Arlington. My first lecture was in Fremont. Exactly at the appointed hour the meeting was called to order. The audience sang "The Church's One Foundation," and I thought I had never before heard such heart-warming, intelligent singing. There was a prayer, and Pastor Wolter introduced me. Here I had my first view of a real Lutheran gathering. As I stood on the stage, there sat before me not a hundred, but several hundred, white people—men, women, and children. I had never seen so many white people in one place before. Was I afraid? No! The Lord Jesus had brought me there. I had an important message to deliver. I had a worthy cause to plead. I was sent there to tell these Christian white people of the deplorable condition of my race in the Alabama field. After I had been introduced, I paused long enough to breathe a prayer, "Lord help me." He did help me, as I could tell from the sympathetic expressions on the faces of those who listened.

From Fremont I continued my lectures at the various places, Seward, Omaha, West Point, Norfolk, David City, Columbus, Bancroft, Blair, Lincoln. I am compelled to say that while I was on this lecture tour I saw the white people in a new light. I am still able to say they are my friends. We colored people have found the dear white Lutheran people to be our friends. We have found neighbors among them like the good Samaritan; we have found teachers among them like those that Christ pointed out as the servants of all; we have found leaders among them like Moses; we have found missionaries among them like the Apostle Paul; we have found among them really God-fearing people. The white Lutherans have a stronger feeling of sympathy for the colored people than the colored people will ever imagine. Oh, that my race could understand the white people! Then they would appreciate more what the white Lutherans are doing for them.

With a joyful and happy heart I turned my face again toward the South, after saying farewell to my gracious host and hostess and their lovely family.

Pastor Schulze had arranged that on my return I should lecture in the Emmaus Church hall in St. Louis. A large audience was assembled. All the members of the Missionary Board except two were present. A large offering was given at that time for starting the work in Africa, which had not yet been begun.

I had so thoroughly enjoyed my stay among the white Lutherans that I longed to get home so that I might relate my experiences to my people. Like a child, I kept asking the porter where we were. Finally, for what seemed a long, long time, the porter did not come through my section of the train. I sat by the window and watched and wondered how near we were to my Alabama home. I saw a truck speeding along the highway, and that truck was labeled, "Ginn, Alabama." I nearly jumped out of my seat. My heart was shouting, "Alabama, Alabama, I am back in Alabama." Soon the train stopped at Snow Hill, and I hurried off to see the friends and relatives who had gathered to greet me on my return. There was also one white friend and my doctor, the late Dr. W. B. Palmer.

Believe me when I say that my story was well related and that all enjoyed hearing about my experiences in the Northland.

After a short rest at home, I attended our annual conference, which convened at Mobile, Ala. Upon my return from the conference I found a letter from Rev. E. G. Hertler, La Crescent, Minn., in which he invited me to come to Minnesota and conduct a lecture tour throughout his conference.

Having received this invitation and a check to cover all expenses, I collected my belongings and started on my way to the beautiful State of Minnesota. This trip took me northwest from Chicago, where I arrived at eight o'clock on a Sunday morning. I believed that I should not disturb Pastor M. N. Carter of our colored church on a Sunday morning; so I sat in the big Union Station until 11:30, when I continued on my journey. At 6:30 in the evening I arrived at La Crosse, Wis., where Pastor Hertler waited to greet me. We hurried on to Onalaska, Minn., where I was to deliver my first lecture. Pastor Bergholz of that congregation had just concluded a day of mission services. His ladies had just finished serving a big dinner. Expecting me to arrive for the evening lecture, they had saved my dinner. And, oh, what a delicious dinner it was, just the kind that white Lutheran ladies always serve!

I thought I was too tired to eat, but when one of the ladies presented me with a large serving of red watermelon, my appetite returned, and I began the destruction of that piece of watermelon. I finished with vim, for all Negroes like watermelons. The melon feast being over, all reassembled to hear my plea for the people of my race. After all the lectures in Nebraska I had become accustomed to speaking to large audiences of white people. It had now become a real pleasure for me to speak to them.

After the evening lecture, Pastor Hertler took me to his home, where I was graciously received by Mrs. Hertler, a true child of God, who does not know her friends by color, race, country, or condition. She possesses the true missionary spirit. I made their home my headquarters for several weeks, but I was never made to feel unwelcome for one moment in the home.

Within the next few days I accompanied Pastor Hertler to the Red Wing Conference at Caledonia, Minn. This was a conference of pastors, teachers, and delegates. In the afternoons the conference suspended all business for a period and gave me the privilege of presenting my cause. I had bravely delivered a series of lectures before thousands of white Lutherans in Nebraska. I dare say you will be surprised when I tell you that I was really nervous when I stood up before this body of men. The occasion was different. The conference was all men, pastors, teachers, professors, doctors, lawyers, bankers, farmers, and other businessmen. I had never faced such well-dressed men. I was the only woman present, and all eyes were focused on me.

Before attempting to make a start, I did as I had always done, I paused long enough to breathe a prayer, "Lord, help me for Jesus' sake." The Lord did help me right then and there. I could soon tell that the hearts of these men were overflowing with sympathy toward me and with profound interest in me and my cause. When I had finished speaking, a short recess was granted, and the time was used to make out my lecture schedule. It was arranged that I should speak each night except Saturday, and sometimes twice on Sundays. The program was given to me for my inspection, and I was asked whether it was too full. I replied: "Let the lamp burn down. That is what it was lighted for—to burn down." The men laughed heartily, and from that time on the ball was rolling easily for all of us.

Each evening I kept my appointment with large audiences and sometimes addressed Sunday schools on Sunday afternoons, Walther League societies, parochial school children, and ladies' aids during the weekdays.

The strain was rather severe, and nature began to demand its revenge for mistreatment. I had to remain in bed the first half of the day. The pastors' wives manifested a great interest in my failing bodily condition. In the morning they brought water and towels to my bed that I might refresh myself for breakfast; then a tray of wholesome breakfast was brought to my bed. After breakfast it was my privilege to fall asleep and to rest until noon, when a fine dinner was brought to me; then I would rise and make preparation to go to the next place. The pastor of the church at which I was to speak always came to get me. It is not easy to lecture every night, to meet different people, different families, eat at a different table, sleep in a different bed. Again some inquired whether the program was too full. I replied: "I told you to let the candle burn down, but you are burning this candle at both ends." The program remained the same.

At one place the church was so large that the pastor spoke of getting a loud-speaker. When he told me what it would cost, I told him I would be the loud-speaker. I spoke at the following places: Onalaska, Hackiah, Caledonia, La Crescent, and Jitzen, Minn.; Nadine, Strausburg, Sparta, La Crosse, Wis.; Winona, Lake City, Zumbrota, Ornoco, Goodhue, Frontenac, Bremen, Red Wing, Rochester, Dexter, Echo, Milville, Austin, Waltham, Claremont, Owatonna, Fairfax, Gibbons, New Ulm, Sleepy Eye, Wood Lake, Renville, Flora, Olivia, Danube, Bellview, Seaforth, St. James, Watertown (3 churches), the Red Wing Conference, the Mississippi Conference, Dr. Martin Luther College, day schools at Austin, Claremont, Fairfax, Des Plaines, and Wood Lake; Sunday school and ladies' aid at Lake City; Sunday school at Emmert; and to congregations in Des Plaines, Chicago (Pastor Carter and Pastor Reinke), and Boyd, Minn.

Before closing this chapter I must write a few lines about the beautiful Northwest. Beneath the western horizon on those western plains are miles and miles of green cornfields. On either side of the road millions of yellow tassels swing in the summer breezes. Here and there are smaller farms. The modern wheatgrower uses huge combines that go through the standing grain, cutting, threshing, delivering the wheat in bags to large trucks that accompany the combines. This section of America produces real wealth. Gold mines, copper mines, and diamond mines are valuable, but they will become exhausted. The wealth of these plains will never be exhausted if the soil is properly cultivated and conserved.

The cities are like most other American cities, filled with busses, filling stations, parking spaces, big stores, movie houses lighted with brilliant lights, beautiful residences, and churches. There are many things and places of interest to charm the traveler. The whole countryside speaks to us of God, who is over us all and who has made the beautiful things for us to enjoy.

Infected teeth brought about a third trip north for me. One day there came a letter to me from a Mrs. Pauline Grootman of Melrose Park, Ill. She related to me that she had had some infected teeth extracted. She inquired whether I had had trouble with my teeth. I answered her affirmatively. Again, I heard from this new friend, who assured me that treatment or extraction of my teeth would work wonders in helping to restore my health. She first discussed my case with her dentist, Dr. Ehlers. He was moved by the Lord to offer his services without charge if I would come to him. Mrs. Grootman wrote again and invited me to her home, saying there would be no charge for my board while I was there. Yet I was unable to accept the offer, for I did not have the money for railroad fare. My pension at that time was fifteen dollars a month.

About this time a deaconess, Katherine Leasch of Watertown, Wis., a friend of Mrs. Grootman, paid the latter a visit. Mrs. Grootman related my case to Deaconess Leasch.

Miss Leasch returned to the Bethesda Lutheran Home at Watertown and informed the teachers. Moved with sympathy, they raised enough for my fare from Snow Hill, Ala., to Chicago. Mrs. Grootman sent me the money. God's hand was working. I wrote a letter of thanks, but felt that I should return the money and not go to Melrose Park. "What is the hindrance now?" Mrs. Grootman asked. I had not secured permission from my superintendent and the Mission Board.

All these years I have tried to obey orders. When my superiors said, "Come," I came; when they said, "Go," I went; and when they said, "Stop," I immediately called a halt. Therefore, not having received orders to go, I refused to accept the offer, even though it would seem to be to my advantage. Mrs. Grootman did not give up, but as soon as she received the explanation of my refusal, she hastened to her telephone and called the Rev. O. C. Boecler at Des Plaines, Ill., who at that time was president of our Mission Board. In that long-distance telephone conversation Pastor Boecler gave his approval for the trip north.

I now had permission from the Board, but the journey was still delayed because I had not informed my superintendent, the Rev. E. A. Westcott, of my desire and plans. After a few days a reply to my letter came from Superintendent Westcott, in which he said: "Go, and may the guardian angel accompany you! I hope you will come back feeling better."

All was ready, and I started on my third trip North, which brought me to Pastor M. N. Carter's home in Chicago, where Mrs. Grootman and Paul Jr. met me. The next day Pastor Carter took me to Dr. Ehlers' office in Oak Park, where I found dear Mrs. Grootman waiting. When the necessary preparations were made for the surgery, both Pastor Carter and Mrs. Grootman prayed. Because the condition of my heart was not good, my home physician had never consented to having my teeth extracted.

Now, there I was sitting in the dentist's chair in Oak Park, Ill. Dr. Ehlers proceeded after the prayer. The doctor extracted ten teeth. Then I became the victim of a severe heart attack. Mrs. Grootman and the pastor still prayed. The prayers were answered. Relief came. I was taken to Mrs. Grootman's home and placed in a quiet room. I soon was well enough to be taken to another dentist to have some necessary fillings made.

I remained in Mrs. Grootman's home one month—without charge. Two dentists had worked without charge. My fare from Snow Hill to Chicago had been provided. Pastor Carter had ministered to me.

Now it was time for me to return home. Pastor C. L. Abel of Elmhurst, Ill., assumed the responsibility and borrowed the money for my fare home. His ladies' aid refunded the full amount.

My health was surely and quickly improving, and I was soon led by the Holy Spirit to offer myself to our Mission Board for active work again. All those I have mentioned in this chapter stand out as good Samaritans to me. All were used as instruments in the hand of God to help bring back my health so that I could again be active in my chosen work. All glory be to Jesus!

19

BACK TO WORK

•

Ye shall be witnesses unto Me
Acts 1:8
The Master is come and calleth for thee
John 11:28

•

MY HEALTH WAS GRADUALLY BECOMING NORMAL. I HAD A
longing to take up my mission work again, but was con-
tinually being discouraged, not only by my physician and
relatives, but by friends and by some of my co-workers.

Day by day, however, the desire to work for Jesus grew
stronger and stronger. My mental picture of all the little
neglected children of my race was revived in my memory.
There was the great commission: "Go ye, therefore, and
teach all nations, baptizing them in the name of the Father
and of the Son and of the Holy Ghost" (Matt. 28:19).

While struggling with the opposing opinions of my fellow
men and the desire of my own heart, the news came that
Pastor Peay, a beloved brother, had been stricken and was
not expected to live. I rushed to his bedside. As I stood at
his bedside, a picture of the whole Alabama field loomed up
before me. Then and there I decided: "I am going back to
work in my mission." Shortly after I had made my decision,
Pastor Peay opened his eyes and looked into my face with a
smile. I told him of my decision to take up my mission work
again. He could not speak, but from the sound of his voice
and his beaming countenance I knew I had his approval.

Thus Pastor Peay was the first to know of my decision to resume my work.

The next ones to be informed were my two brothers, Teacher S. U. Young and S. L. Young, both of Snow Hill, Ala. They gave me strong words of encouragement. When I told a cousin of my mother of my plans, her comment was: "Are you going back to tramping again?" There wasn't much encouragement in such words, but I took it with a smile, as I always try to do when things are said that make me feel bad. I answered: "Oh, don't call it tramping! I am going back to save souls for Jesus."

By this time the news had spread, and I began to receive all kinds of advice from co-workers, relatives, and friends, both white and colored. Even my physician was sure I was not able to undertake such a thing.

After spending many wakeful nights in prayer, my application to the Missionary Board was drawn up and sent through the Selma office, which at that time was under the supervision of Superintendent E. A. Westcott.

The Missionary Board informed me that the application had been received and that according to the superintendent's recommendation they would ask me to go to Ingomar. Ingomar had been as a sick child for many years, and they desired that I go there to see whether anything could be done. To accept the call meant nothing to me but a hard life of sacrifice and suffering because of the living conditions. Co-workers, pastors, relatives, and friends spoke against my going.

I tell you, dear reader, I did not get a thrill out of going to Ingomar. My father, 86 years old, was paralyzed; but when the time came for me to go to Ingomar, I gave up father, house, home, and went in the name of Jesus and for His cause. I gave up all my earthly goods save my clothes and my books. I said: "You may have all the world, but give me Jesus."

Ingomar is located on the Alabama River, in what is called the lower end of Dallas County. It was twelve miles from any store, twenty miles from a railroad, fifteen miles from the nearest physician, forty-four miles from Selma, the county seat. The people of that community were so far removed from every modern improvement that the only late invention the people ever saw were the airplanes flying high in the sky.

Only two cars came that way, the rural mail carrier's car and our pastor's car. If anyone else ever traveled the road from Minter to Ingomar, his appearance was almost a show for the people of the countryside.

If we wanted to buy anything, we had to meet the "Rolling Store" as the big truck was called that passed through at very irregular intervals, loaded with old goods. Since it often came on Sunday, I was seldom able to patronize the "Rolling Store."

The people had no timepieces. If by chance I permitted my watch to run down, the only way I could get the time was to wait for the mail carrier on the road.

When the Alabama River overflowed its banks, we were, indeed, cut off from everything until the waters subsided, unless we could move out. This happened once in the year I was there. The people offered to take me out, but I preferred to remain.

The people lived in neighborhoods called "quarters." These quarters were far apart, and I was not able to walk from one quarter to another as I could have done in previous years. Therefore, in order to make visits away from my own quarter, I had to send out for a car and a chauffeur. Though the charge was a dollar an hour, the car might stop running at any time, and then I would have to pay for the hours spent in the repair shop. This cut deep into my salary of $35.00 a month.

People of this community suffered much from chills, malaria, and typhoid. Finally I fell a victim to chills and fever. There was no doctor. The people treated me with a tea which they made from a yellow weed blossom. They gave me so much of the tea that I was almost deaf for several days. By a letter I succeeded in getting in touch with my pastor, Rev. G. A. Williston, who came and took me to a doctor. When Superintendent Westcott heard of my illness, he came to get me, but by that time I had improved sufficiently to remain at Ingomar.

Was anything accomplished at Ingomar? I would answer, "Not much." When I went to Grace Congregation at Ingomar, there was only one member left, a man who by his outward life plainly showed that he had very little love for Jesus in his heart. With the aid of the Holy Spirit and with the physical strength I had I put up a hard fight, but the battle was a losing one. I enrolled 84 in the day school. Out of this number I won one young boy for confirmation, and the promise of several children for Baptism. The boy was confirmed after I left, but the other children were never baptized.

When my school closed in the spring, I was called home to the bedside of my father. He lived one month after I came home. I did not return to Ingomar. I felt that I had done all I could, and I so informed the superintendent, but I added that if it was the Lord's will for me to return, I was willing to go.

The Rev. J. T. Skinner was called and served the congregation one year, but because the people of Ingomar rejected

•

the pure Gospel, Grace Congregation disbanded, and the building was sold to the Good Shepherd Congregation at Vineland.

In the year in which I resigned at Ingomar the superintendent came to me saying: "It is feared that eventually Mt. Carmel at Midway will have to be closed, and the Mission Board is asking you to go back to Midway, your old stamping ground, to see what can be done." Having a burning zeal to be a witness for Christ wherever I was needed, I answered the call.

I had served Midway before; in fact, I had helped to organize the mission there, but I had been away fifteen years, and during that time Midway had gone through many changes with many ups and downs, mostly downs. At one time there was a large school at Midway, and a large church membership. It ranked among the leading stations on our field. When I returned, nearly all those who had been there in the early days had moved away. Only four of the older families still remained. Only two members of the congregation remained who had been there during my fifteen years' stay. Others had joined whom I did not know. The people who had moved in were an entirely different class of people. They were living as if the season of grace would never end for them. They were sinful, even immoral. They spent their time in idle living, drinking, gambling, picking their banjos at wild, sinful frolics. The superintendent often referred to Midway as the modern Sodom.

I arrived at Midway in the early fall. The whole plantation seemed to be grown up in weeds and bushes. Only the tops of the houses could be seen from a distance. The roofs were falling in, the yards and houses were filthy.

The old road leading to the church was overgrown with tall grass; parts of the road were washed into big ruts. The fine church building which had been erected in memory of Albert Woelfle had been torn down, and only a small chapel was left. The beautiful church furniture, the altar and pulpit, the baptismal font had been severely abused. The neat little collection table had been taken from its place in the church. The organ was gone.

Fortunately a fine young man and his wife, Lutherans from childhood, still lived in the community, and their home was opened to me, and I was made most welcome. They, Mr. and Mrs. C. L. Rawls, with their family of six children, are still helping to keep the church at Midway.

On the first Sunday I was first to reach the little church. I stood on the church steps to greet all who would come. The pastor was the next to arrive. Very soon I was able to discern that the pastor, Rev. G. S. Roberts, was somewhat discouraged. The hour came for service. A few children were there, but not one adult, not even my host and hostess. Six or eight pennies made up the Sunday school offering.

The day came for the school to open. About thirty-five came to be enrolled. But it was reported that the patrons did not expect to pay the tuition fee of one dollar nor buy books for their children. I finally persuaded them to pay. They agreed under the condition that they be given the full seven months in which to pay. When I began to talk about books, one father said: "Miss Rosa, dese here chillun ain't goin' to learn nothin', and I'm not about to buy no books." What should I do? I ordered all that would be needed and paid for them out of my own salary. When the parents and children saw the new books, they really wanted to possess some of them. Some paid a little of the cost of the books, while others sent sweet potatoes, eggs, and nuts to help pay for the "pretty" books. Even though I did get more sweet potatoes than I needed, I was willing to accept whatever was brought in order that the children might have their books. But the tablets and pencils I had to buy and pay for.

Now you wonder how things worked out. I remained at Midway nine years, and before I left I was able to collect just about all the tuition in advance, and all the money for books. The children even paid for all the pencils and paper they needed.

Through the day school we were able to build up the Sunday school. Before we could organize any classes for instruction, we had to persuade the people to make the first necessary preparation. Only four couples on this large plantation were married. They merely lived together. By the grace of God we succeeded in getting several couples married, and they joined instruction classes; some for confirmation, and some for Baptism.

During my first term I succeeded in getting along until Christmas without being ill. Then one day in the schoolroom I was stricken with a heart attack. The children managed somehow to get me to my room. The doctor was called. Pastor and Mrs. Roberts spent the whole night by my side. I was not expected to live. I should not fail to say that on this occasion it was the white manager of this large plantation who befriended me. The young son drove the ten miles to Camden to bring the doctor and even paid the bill. Everyone did everything that could be done for me. The superintendent was informed of my illness, and when I was not soon able to return to the school, he secured a helper for me, Miss Annie Myree. She taught a month. I then attempted to take over, but the children did more of the teaching than

I, for I was exhausted by the time the morning devotions and the class in religion were conducted. At the end of this eventful year I was asked to remain at Midway. I could easily see that there was plenty for me to do.

There was no well in the churchyard, and this was a great hindrance to the work; so during that summer, on my own responsibility, I had a well dug. Finally the men agreed that we should have the well, and that they would dig it. The women were to provide the dinners. Twenty men came together to do the digging, and on the fifth day water was found. The young white man who had paid the doctor bill for me gave enough lumber to curb the well and to build a shelter over it. We all rejoiced that the well was finished. But my summer's work was not finished. I now went from house to house in the hot August sun to get the men to build a bridge over the stream that crossed the road to the chapel. Often services could not be held because the water was too high to cross either with the car or on foot. The public road superintendent gave the lumber for the bridge, and the men did the work. Now that the busy vacation was over, we were ready to begin another year of school. This term I was given a permanent helper for my school. Then it was decided to send a different one each year or second year so that some special mission training might be given the young women before they went out to teach alone. During the nine years these were the girls who worked with me: Annie Davis, Lydia Mae Davis, Icie Lee White, Ludy Dunning, and Wincie Jackson.

In order that living conditions might be easier and more pleasant for us, the Mission Board had a teacherage built on the grounds. They even provided me with a horse and buggy. I was happy, even though I did have to spend many nights alone. My comfort and contentment were always in these words: "I will be with you." When illness overtook me, the Lord always had someone near to help me. It was understood that if the school bell rang during the night or at an unusual hour, help was needed at the teacherage, and the people always came, sometimes a score of them. I even enjoyed having the horse and buggy, until one day the horse became afraid and ran away, throwing both me and the other teacher out. I received only a few bruises and the other teacher a broken arm, but the buggy was almost ruined. So it was that my walking started again.

Then the bridge did not hold up. Something else had to be done so that the children could get to school without wading the water. Finally the men on the plantation agreed to build a pole walk (a walk made of small logs) over the swampy part of the road. This was not very satisfactory, but it was better than none, even though the children and I often had to get out with boots on to keep the logs from floating away. Thus there was always something difficult to do. My friends wondered why I should stay on. I tried to see the pleasant side always, and I would sometimes say to those who urged me to leave: "I may have to stay here until I die. This may be my reward for bringing the Lutheran Church into Alabama, but if it is, I take comfort in knowing that my Father is getting ready a reward in heaven." Once I asked to be moved, and the reply was that "the little plant I had started was not strong enough to be left." I took fresh courage to go on.

But the people were always moving in and moving out, and the moving out always took some of our members away. These things were hard to bear, but there were pleasant things, too. Several white friends from the North visited me during my stay, among them: Mr. and Mrs. Ernst of Wisconsin, Misses Margaret and Bertha Wunderlich, and Mr. and Mrs. W. H. Wunderlich of Pittsburgh, and Mr. and Mrs. Ahlbrand of Seymour, Ind. These friends gave me much encouragement, and often brought me rich gifts.

With all the hardships, I knew that I was about my Father's business and Jesus was with me. The term of service at Midway came to an end, but my heart is still with the few faithful members who are striving to keep the Sunday school and church services and even the Christian day school.

20

HOME AGAIN

•

*I am with thee and will keep thee in all places whither thou
goest and will bring thee again into this land*
GEN. 28:15

•

GOD'S TIME HAD COME TO BRING ME BACK HOME. ONE DAY
before leaving Midway, I looked out and saw Superintendent
Ellwanger coming. He had left his car on the other side of
the pond and had walked across on the poles. It was always
a most pleasant surprise to see someone coming, for I was
very much isolated from the rest of the workers. And this time
the superintendent had come to ask whether I wanted to stay
at Midway. To me that was a strange question, for after nine
years I had almost come to believe I would stay there the rest
of my days. Others before me had resigned rather than remain
in such a difficult place, but I could not entertain such a
thought; therefore, if no call came, I was willing to stay.

My reply to the superintendent's question was: "Because of
my age and my health, and because of the living conditions
here, I would not like to remain, but if you want me to stay,
I will."

Then he mentioned Pine Hill, Rosebud, and Selma, but
asked me not to fix my mind on any one of these places, for
it had not yet been decided where I should serve. The hint of
such a possibility gave me to know that God's hand was
working and He had not forgotten me. His hand was stretched
out still.

The next week there came a knock at the door of the little teacherage, and when I opened the door, there stood the superintendent again. He had come to ask me to go to Rosebud to conduct a vacation Bible school. Within a few days I was happily settled in the teacherage there. My joy at being back at my "old home" was almost indescribable.

The next day was Sunday. I went to church and sat between my sister and a dear friend, but I could not restrain the tears. Why was I weeping? I was thinking of the time thirty years before when in good faith I had left my father's house, given up my school, my church, my friends, and had gone out to prepare the way for the establishment of the Lutheran Church among my people. I was thinking of the obstacles, the difficulties, and the hardships I had faced for my Savior. Now, after thirty long years, I was again at home. I wept as I recalled all these things.

The congregation at Rosebud was making preparations to celebrate its thirtieth anniversary. I fell in line to help. The ladies' aid worked almost day and night to be ready for this great occasion. June 16, 1946, was a memorable day, when a great number of Lutherans gathered in the mother Church to celebrate the coming of Lutheranism to Alabama.

Superintendent W. H. Ellwanger preached the morning sermon. In the afternoon the sermon was preached by the Rev. G. A. Schmidt, now pastor of the First English Lutheran Church in New Orleans. It was a real joy to the people to greet and to hear again the voice of their beloved former superintendent. Next to God, the Christian day schools in Alabama owe their existence to Pastor Schmidt.

After this great day had been so successfully ended, it was time for the vacation Bible school. I spent four happy weeks in this school.

Like a thunderbolt out of a clear sky came another call, this time to the Alabama Lutheran Academy at Selma. I was already as happy at Rosebud as I ever expected to be in this life. I desired nothing better on this earth. The people were happy to have me return, and I was happy to be working again in the school where I had taught thirty years before and where I was born. I had hoped that I might remain here until the end of my days on earth.

Excitement ran high over this call. Even my pastor was opposed to my leaving Rosebud. The members sent letters to the superintendent's office to plead that I might be permitted to remain. The white people whom I had known through these many years expressed their regret and hoped that I might stay. Then the pastor came to say that I would be permitted to make my own decision, and if I chose to remain at Rosebud, that would settle the matter. I could not make such a decision alone. I went to my heavenly Father and asked Him what to do. I prayed almost constantly. I fell asleep praying, and when I awoke, my first thought was a prayer. I went into the church, and down on my knees before the altar I poured out my heart to God. I did not wish to make a mistake. I had no rest, no peace, until I decided to go to Selma. I began to pack my suitcases at once. The hour had come for the visit of my pastor and Superintendent Ellwanger. I wanted once more to go into the church to pray before they should arrive; but as I left my house, I saw young David Ellwanger, the son of the superintendent, approaching. I said to myself: "The die is cast."

After a happy greeting we all went into the church together. The call was explained again. We talked at length, and the superintendent prayed. By this time I was sure of my decision. The pastor gave me his blessing. My things, already packed, were placed in the superintendent's car and taken along to Selma.

The following day, Sunday, the people came to church, still greatly excited. The pastor sought to comfort them and to show them the need for my going.

I have not lived on flowery beds of ease since I came to Selma. There have been difficulties to overcome. The work has been new and different. I had to win the confidence of the students and of my co-workers. It seems to me that nothing has been left undone to make my work at the academy easy and pleasant. If it is the Lord's will, I shall be happy to spend the rest of my days here, helping the boys and girls who are preparing for the holy ministry and for teaching in our Christian day schools.

Pray for me that I may continue in the faith of my dear Lutheran Church, so that when civilization shall confess, like a weary traveler upon a dusty road, "I have gone as far as I can"; when all the achievements of mankind shall have crumbled beneath the ironclad hoofs of time and time itself shall be swallowed up in the vast sea of eternity, even thus, as you sit by the river of life making sweet melody with your heavenly harps, I, with thousands of colored people whom God will have led from the spiritual darkness in the Black Belt of Alabama, can be heard singing praises to Jesus, the Savior of sinners, whom I have learned to know so well through His Word in our Lutheran Zion. If the Lutheran Church had not come into Alabama and led us out of spiritual darkness into the light of God's Word, where would we have been?

Thou, whose almighty Word
Chaos and darkness heard
　　And took their flight;
Hear us, we humbly pray,
And where the Gospel day
Sheds not its glorious ray,
　　"Let there be light!"

Thou, who didst come to bring,
On Thy redeeming wing,
   Healing and sight,
Health to the sick in mind,
Sight to the inly blind,
Oh, now to all mankind
   "Let there be light!"

Spirit of Truth and Love,
Life-giving holy Dove,
   Speed forth Thy flight.
Move on the waters' face,
Bearing the lamp of grace,
And in earth's darkest place
   "Let there be light!"

Holy and blessed Three,
Glorious Trinity,
   Wisdom, Love, Might!
Boundless as ocean's tide
Rolling in fullest pride,
Through the earth, far and wide,
   "Let there be light!"

APPENDIX

MISSIONARIES WHO HAVE LABORED
ON THE ALABAMA FIELD

•

*Go ye, therefore, and teach all nations, baptizing them in the name
of the Father and of the Son and of the Holy Ghost*
MATT. 28:19

•

The Sainted Rev. Nils J. Bakke.—Pastor Bakke was the
man whom God used to unfurl the banner of Lutheranism
in the Dark Belt and turn on the true light of the Gospel.
His life and work have been dwelt upon at length in this
volume. "Blessed are the dead which die in the Lord from
henceforth; yea, saith the Spirit, that they may rest from
their labors, and their works do follow them."

The Rev. G. A. Schmidt was a true friend to all on the
Alabama field. He was a God-fearing man, a faithful servant
of Jesus during his years of service among my people, and he
is still our friend, though he labors in another field.

No night was too dark, no wind too chilly nor rough, no
rain too heavy, no sun too hot, no sand too deep, no mud too
treacherous, no house too dirty, no family too poor, and no
person too ignorant for him to go to carry the Gospel of
Jesus, the Master. He was kind to all, patient with all, con-
siderate of all, true to his friends. He was easy to approach. A
little child could stop him. To him we give the credit for the
organization of our Alabama Lutheran school system. His
work will never die.

The Rev. E. A. Westcott—I feel somewhat like the Apostle Paul before King Agrippa (Acts 26:2). I think myself
happy, dear friends, to have the opportunity to speak for this

196

servant of the Lord. I believe with all my heart there has never been a missionary in our midst more interested in colored mission work than Pastor Westcott. He labored among us twenty-five years with an untiring devotion to the cause. He not only would go one mile, or two miles, but he would go all the way to help someone. I never knew him to turn away a colored person who needed help. He was a faithful steward, though sometimes misunderstood.

The Rev. Wm. G. Kennell is a man of implicit faith and trust in God. His highest delight and joy is to work in the Negro mission field. The fruits of his labors are many. He is the present editor of the *Missionary Lutheran.*

The Rev. Walter H. Ellwanger is our present superintendent. He came/to us at a very difficult time; for since the organization of our churches there has been a great falling away. "For that day shall not come except there come a falling away first" (2 Thess. 2:3); "And because iniquity shall abound, the love of many shall wax cold" (Matt. 24:12). There truly has been a mighty falling away, but we comfort ourselves with the thought that the work is the Lord's, and He has sent us again a consecrated man to be our leader. Pastor Ellwanger is a man of prayer, a man of faith, a man of methods, a man of thought. As director of Alabama Lutheran Academy he is doing much to help the young boys and girls who come here to study.

The Rev. Wm. H. Jones' name stands high among those of white missionaries who have come to Alabama. He is now pastor of Faith Lutheran Church in Mobile. Among his members he is regarded as a true servant of the Lord.

Mr. E. H. Dahlke was with us only one short year, but he was highly respected by all his co-workers and the students.

He leaves us with the promise that if God wills it, he will return to work on the Alabama field.

Pastors Eckert, Kreft, Krause, Drier, Wicker, and Wolf, served at different times on the Alabama field but accepted calls into other fields. On every hand people are calling for the Gospel light, and other fields must be served as well as the Alabama field for the colored.

The Rev. I. S. Holness came to us from England to be pastor and teacher at Alabama Lutheran Academy, later to serve in the Eastern field, where he fell asleep in Jesus. His body lies buried in Atlanta, Ga., many miles from his homeland.

The Rev. W. H. Lane was the first colored pastor called by the Missionary Board to the Alabama field. He served for brief periods at Rosebud and Vredenburgh.

The Rev. M. N. Carter, D.D., served at Rosebud and Possum Bend. Pastor Carter is a forceful preacher of the Gospel, a man of keen intellect, an orator of no mean reputation. He is now serving the Lord among the Lutheran colored brethren in Chicago.

The Rev. R. O. L. Lynn, better known as Professor Lynn, served as pastor at Vredenburgh, at Buena Vista, and at Tinela. He was the first president of Alabama Luther College, now Alabama Lutheran Academy. Being a profound scholar himself, he has always been deeply interested in the advancement of his own race. As a teacher and director of school affairs, he has always been held in the highest respect by students and co-workers.

The late *Rev. Charles Peay* was for many years a true counselor for pastors, teachers, and for lay members of the Lutheran Church in Alabama. He was chairman of the Alabama Conference at the time of his untimely departure from this life. He inspired many young men and women to higher ideals. His remains repose in God's acre at Mt. Calvary Church, Tilden, Ala.

The *Rev. E. R. Berger* labored at Joffre, Holy Ark, Tilden, and Ingomar and was later called to Alexandria, La., where he still serves the Lord of the Church.

The *Rev. P. D. Lehman* taught for several years in Alabama Lutheran Academy before he was called to Los Angeles.

The *Rev. Wm. T. Eddleman* serves Pilgrim Church in Birmingham, the only self-supporting church in the Alabama field.

The *Rev. H. J. Lehman* succeeded the sainted Pastor Peay as chairman of the Alabama Lutheran Conference. He served as pastor at Selma, at Rosebud and Oak Hill until 1946, when he was called to St. Matthew's Church (colored) in Baltimore.

The *Rev. G. S. Roberts* served 13 years as pastor at Catherine and Midway. He was called in May, 1947, to begin work among the colored in Chattanooga, Tenn.

The *Rev. Wm. Schweppe,* while on furlough from his work in Africa, served on the Gulf Coast. He endeared himself to the people, especially by his lectures on the work in Africa.

In 1948 our pastors in Alabama were:

Rev. A. Dominick, Montrose and Maysville

Rev. R. E. Neely, Buena Vista, Tinela, Vredenburgh, and Longmile

Rev. W. J. Pledger, Possum Bend, Tait's Place, and Rockwest

Rev. J. T. Skinner, Oak Hill and Rosebud

Rev. E. H. Thompson, Arlington, Nyland, Lamison, and Pine Hill

Rev. S. L. Gailes, Vineland and Bashi

Rev. R. F. Jenkins, Trinity, Selma, and St. Timothy, E. Selma

Rev. P. R. Hunt, King's Landing

Rev. R. L. Graeber, Joffre, Holy Ark, and Maplesville

Rev. Wm. H. Jones, Mobile, Atmore, Freemansville

Rev. Wm. G. Kennell, Pensacola and Oakfield, Fla; Pascagoula, Miss.

Vacant, Catherine, Midway, Tilden, Camden, Ackerville, and Hamburg

The names of Hazberg, Bates, Harts, Grigsby, Johnson, Means, Cozart, S. Tervalon, Montgomery, and Carlson are familiar to those who know the history of the Alabama field.